Graduation
Life Lessons of a Professional Footballer

by Richard Lee

Published by Bennion Kearny Limited
6 Victory House, 64 Trafalgar Road
Birmingham, B13 8BU

www.BennionKearny.com

Cover image: ©Mark Fuller
Inside images: ©Mark Fuller unless otherwise shown. A number of images are courtesy of Richard Lee and Action Images. Contact Bennion Kearny for specific details.

Acknowledgements

I guess this is the perfect opportunity to thank a few people who have had a huge influence on me and my life; admittedly I rarely tell them, so hopefully this will win me some brownie points!

I've had several influential people in my life who have all played their part in helping me gain the knowledge and understanding to not only write this book but allowed me the opportunity to lead a fulfilling life with such promise and hope for the future.

To name a few:

Holly - your support and understanding has always been a huge factor in my achievements. You are beautiful, so kind and will always hold a special place within me.

Mum - You've always sacrificed a lot for me and my brothers, we may not always show it but we do appreciate everything you do and know that all you do is with us in mind.

Dad - My biggest motivation is to emulate the success you've achieved and allow my future family to have the same opportunities that you've given me. You have been my biggest influence.

Brothers - I like that we've grown closer over the years, you are all incredibly talented (except at football) and I have no doubt exciting times await.

Daren - our daily discussions are a source of inspiration and I'm convinced we help push each other to great things, you are a true friend.

Bob - you are the inspiration behind me writing this book, you have helped open my eyes to what can be achieved and I'm delighted to have had the opportunity to become a good friend of yours.

Keith - I continue to learn from you with every discussion we have, such wisdom. You helped set me upon this journey I find myself on and for that I'll be eternally grateful.

Dave Sabat - You were the missing element for me last season, which upon discovering allowed me to excel, it's not often I meet like-minded people so I'm delighted to have met you.

Zoe - you help organise my life and allow me to pursue ideas I would ordinarily never have the chance to do. I'm very lucky to have you.

I must give a mention to the various physiotherapists that have helped rebuild me on several occasions, namely: Andy Rolls, Phil Edwards, Richard Collinge, Luke Anthony and Neil Greig. As well as several fantastic goalkeeping coaches, whose knowledge has helped shaped my game: Kevin Hitchcock, Alec Chamberlain, Colin Barnes and Simon Royce I thank you all sincerely.

Other close friends: David Hunt, Martin Coll, and Carl Gunning, I consider myself fortunate to be associated with you.

I've been privileged enough to meet so many great people in my life, dating back to my school days, many team-mates throughout the years, and now in my role at Brentford FC. Far too many to mention but to all those who are close to me, who show support via the various social links, and who help energise me in so many different ways - I thank you sincerely.

Rich

About Mark Fuller

Many of the images in this book are the work of Mark D. Fuller. Mark is Brentford FC's Official Photographer, currently in his fifth season - fulfilling the role having missed only a handful of friendly games during that time. Shooting 750-1500 frames per game, each season racks up around 50,000 shots and about 15,000 miles of travel. Keeping up with these demands is a collection of Canon professional photography equipment and a battered Audi A6.

Mark's Brentford FC work can be viewed at officialbfcpics.co.uk Official Brentford picture updates are on Twitter: @BFCPics Mark also undertakes product photography for a number of clients including the Premier League and Championship football clubs.

Other photography work undertaken includes Corporate and PR work along with the occasional wedding. Mark's non football work is featured at www.markdfuller.co.uk and if you need a photographer then he can be contacted by email: mark@markdfuller.co.uk
Follow Mark on Twitter: @TheMarkFuller.

Preface

My name is Richard Lee. I am a goalkeeper and I have played football professionally for 10 years and counting.

The majority of my career has been spent with Watford FC, I joined them at a young age and remained a 'Hornet' until the age of 27, apart from a brief stint at Blackburn Rovers. In 2010 I joined Brentford FC, with whom I still ply my trade.

My career to date hasn't been extraordinary in terms of what I've achieved by any means. I have played in the Premier League, but only 11 games. I've played many times in the Championship and more recently League One. My biggest game to date was my appearance in an FA Cup semi-final - one we lost convincingly to Manchester United - a big day but certainly not one that will make a happy ending in a Disney film.

My career details only tell a small part of my tale, one that dates back to when I donned the gloves as a 9 year old. I joined Watford a year later and it soon became apparent that I had a chance to progress as a goalkeeper. Coaches seemed to take to me and I had many attributes that suggested I could have a worthwhile career in the game.

Now before I carry on I think it's important that you know something. The truth is that I don't love football, I never have. I often get asked the question and respond on autopilot 'I love football, football means everything to me'. It doesn't, and I'll explain why.

The majority of my footballing career has been one of emotional turmoil. I would succumb to chronic nerves before games. I endured serious injuries that led me to consider *what I do* many times over the years before eventually deciding to carry on (with everyone else telling me how lucky I was 'to be doing something I loved'). Surely doing something you loved shouldn't make you feel physically sick for 50 days of each year? I could always appreciate their perspective but this wasn't the reason I carried on. For me football offered the ultimate challenge to myself. If I were to quit - it would be due to a lack of understanding about me and my emotions, a lack of understanding that allowed self-doubt and a lack of confidence to prosper. Surely this would then crop up again at some point in my life? Would I quit again? Probably.

Knowing that it was either a case of quitting or learning to master my emotions I decided to dedicate my time to learning about what makes us tick and how we are best able to perform at the very highest level. After reading hundreds of books on the mind, attending seminars and more recently gaining a qualification in the field of NLP (Neuro Linguistic Programming) I just completed my most outstanding season to date and I know it's no coincidence.

The season I speak of was 2010/11, my first season as a Brentford FC player. It was as if someone presented me with a variety of the exact challenges I needed to overcome in order to know I'd finally gained an understanding of the workings of my mind. Funnily enough the season itself will be considered relatively mediocre by many a Brentford fan but for me this season changed my life.

I'm not sure what the remainder of my career has in store for me but I'm content in that I now realise I've done what I set out to do, and I'm now ready for the next step in my life - whenever that may come. Football has never been my life or even a game against an opponent, for me football has been a game against myself, a profession that has taught me more about myself than any book ever could.

This book tells the tale of what was a turbulent season but more so the culmination of lessons learnt from some incredible mentors, mixed in with experiences over the past 10 years in professional football. They have helped shape what I now consider to be a highly productive strategy in the pursuit of success in any arena.

It's taken me 10 years but I feel as though I've finally won.

Table of Contents

1

June
A Hornet to a Bee

The summer of 2010 would go down as one of my more unsettling ones; out of contract and technically unemployed as of July - I had to make a tough decision with regards to my football career.

I wasn't overly excited by the prospect of another season sat on the bench at Watford but for a long time this looked like my only option. I certainly didn't have enough money to consider other avenues and I was well aware that even a sub-par football contract would far outweigh anything I could get in the 'real world'. I was also well aware that on the face of it I had a fantastic job, I got paid to keep fit, or more accurately in my case I got paid in exchange for the gradual deterioration of my body which that summer in particular I was quite conscious of.

Forgotten man

There wasn't much in terms of making a decision for most of the summer. Watford had offered a one year extension that had seen financial terms reduced by 30% on the previous year. Quite a heavy reduction, but one I could understand. I had barely played, apart from two cup games, and had spent an entire season on the bench. With the recession that had engulfed the world, now hitting football, I fully understood their decision. Why pay me when the impact I have is limited? The world of football now, and goalkeeping in particular, is becoming tougher; if Watford were desperate for a goalkeeper they could loan someone in on short notice and save a fortune by not having a well-paid number two. It just makes business sense. Despite understanding this I was, however, disappointed by the situation. I had served the club for 17 years and despite the promise of an extension (from as early as December) it took until April to come, and when it did it was unexpectedly reduced. The reality check was that I was no longer the 'asset' I once was.

I hadn't ever previously entered into my final year of a contract, and certainly not the last few months. This was never an issue when I was travelling with the England Under-21 squad, or playing in the Premiership as a 24 year old. Now it was my club 'doing me a favour'. If I was to turn down this offer - there may not be another.

Time to think

One thing that did work in my favour was that the Watford manager at the time - Malky Mackay - had shown some sensitivity in allowing me a few extra weeks to decide as to whether I would sign or not. As I weighed up my options - signing an extension seemed like the safest thing to do. Having not played for so long I had, in truth, vacated the radar of many managers.

Leaving Watford would mean a further cut in wages and I wasn't guaranteed that any club would even take me, what with the number of unemployed footballers growing at an alarming rate. The issue at Watford was simply that I wasn't playing. Ideally I needed to get away because if I had another season similar to 2009/2010 - I may have left it too late. There would be plenty of other unemployed goalkeepers who would have played far more games than the 110 I had played. I could sense I was getting into a dangerous situation, very comfortable but disappearing game-by-game into the goalkeeping black hole. I knew I had something to offer but with goalkeeper Scott Loach performing well at Watford my chance did not look like it would come any time soon.

It's not what you know...

It was a rather innocuous phone conversation with a close friend of many years - David Hunt - who was plying his trade at Brentford that got the ball rolling. Brentford FC had shown interest in me a year before but Watford did not let me leave. Instead, Brentford had opted for Lewis Price, who suffered a tough time, before the club loaned in Wojciech Szczezny from Arsenal, with Szcezny gaining rave reviews for his time at Griffin Park. Back on the phone conversation with David, I informed him of my wages and left things with him. A meeting with Andy Scott, Brentford FC's manager, was arranged soon after.

Back at Watford, I was open with Malky, and although he made it clear that he needed to know soon - as my departure would mean Watford FC needing to bring in a keeper - he understood my position. In football, loyalty can count for little, but I felt that given my history with Watford a few extra days to make a decision wouldn't hurt. Thankfully they agreed.

Chapter 1 - June

First impressions

The plan was to meet Andy Scott in Croydon, at a Costa Coffee. I made the journey with my agent and rather than my usual attire of flip flops and jeans I decided to make an effort – boots and jeans. I would quite happily have worn flip flops but these boots gave me an extra couple of inches in height. Knowing that part of the job description of the modern goalkeeper is 'Giant' I felt this to be important. In fact, this was an issue that had plagued me several times throughout my career. For the record I am 6ft, which is frustrating seeing that my dad stands at 6ft4, and my three brothers are all of 6ft2+. And none of them even like football! People often think of me as being smaller but I think that's because I tend to 'play low', my belief being that I can exert more power from a lower stance than others.

Height wasn't an issue at school!
(Pictured in the middle at the back).

Andy turned up, he was well dressed and we all struck up conversation instantly. I have always been quite confident of myself in these situations. I would compare it to meeting a girlfriend's parents; it doesn't take a genius to know what they are looking for. Simply being polite, having a broad smile, and positivity can get you a long way! I had to adapt these methods slightly but it helped in that I was confident in what I had to say.

I know goalkeeping; I have studied it since the age of 8. Even now when I watch football I don't watch the outfield players, I watch the goalkeepers and can assess their game to the smallest detail. My knowledge of outfield players is dreadful but I have no interest in this. I often have to blag my way through conversations when asked which outfield player performed well to which I'll often use the same method. I compliment a striker who scored, or praise a defence if they've kept a clean sheet (midfielders tend to miss out when I analyse). But if someone was to ask me about goalkeeping then they had better have a few minutes to spare. The only issue with this is that I am hypercritical and that includes being hypercritical towards myself. I expect perfection and in the past have experienced severe frustration when I have been anything but. More about that later.

The conversation went as expected, I liked Andy, he appeared genuine and the results he had gained in the previous two years spoke for themselves. He was considered a bright young manager, one who had a big future ahead of him and I was excited by the prospect of seeing what ideas he had for managing the football club, and the club's players. I laboured on the point of how I 'liked feedback' so that I knew what I could offer to best suit a manager. Andy was in full agreement. I also thought it best to inform him of the various injuries I had picked up during my time to which he showed sensitivity. The joint goal was that I would play 50 games that year, and in order to do this I would need to be careful in what training I did.

Leaving the meeting I knew we would receive a call within a day or two with a contract offer - we did.

Decision time

Unsurprisingly the contract offered was exactly the same as the one Watford had offered. The basic wage was matched exactly, the only difference being that the appearance fee I received for sitting on the bench at Watford was now what I would get for making a full appearance at Brentford. And naturally the win bonuses in League One were much smaller than in the Championship.

I had been with Watford FC for two thirds of my life but this was an easy decision for two reasons. One, the opportunity to get myself back on the goalkeeping map. Two, Brentford offered me a two year contract. Security - signed and sealed.

Little did I know what the following season would bring. I had just taken my seat on the roller coaster and pulled down the safety harness. No turning back now.

2

July
The New Boy at School

I was amongst several new arrivals on day one. There would be no formal introductions but I knew David Hunt and he certainly helped integrate me into the group, which I was thankful for.

I had first met David as a 15 year old. Quite randomly he started dating a girl who I sat next to on the way to school each day. David and I shared similar interests, and we grew close and soon found ourselves attending England Youth training camps together. At the time David played for Crystal Palace and I was at Watford. As luck would have it we played against each other in what was (for both of us) only our second ever professional games. The game finished 1-0 to us. The goal scorer? An own goal from David, something I wouldn't let him live down for a while!

Being candid, my first impressions of Brentford were unimpressive to say the least. There were changing rooms that had not had any attention for thirty years, a portable cabin was the physiotherapy room, and someone had innovatively integrated the gym and canteen area into one! Just in case you couldn't decide whether you wanted to do bicep curls or eat a sandwich, well the club could cater for either/or simultaneously. And as you can imagine, there is nothing more appetising than eating that sandwich with a sweaty footballer on the exercise bike next to you or the regular occurrence of a stray football from the gym hitting you on the back of the head during lunch. First impressions did not quite match the big picture that had been painted prior to my arrival.

On a positive note I began to become acquainted with some of my new team mates and there was a nice vibe around the dressing room. I would describe it as a 'down to earth' feel to the place; there were no prima donnas, and a few characters that instantly stood out: Sam Saunders for his bubbly nature, for example. In turn, Mickey Spillane and Myles Weston were forever on each other's case (in a playful way) although Mickey would regularly overstep the mark to the point that it became expected and was instantly forgiven. It also became clear early on that David Hunt was the practical joker. In fellow goalkeeper Simon Moore I could see glimpses of myself as a young pro - fantastic attitude and potential to match.

Something that was instantly apparent as a difference between Watford and Brentford was the contents of the club's car park. There may only be one division between the clubs but the gulf between the Championship and League One is large financially, with the average wage in League One being around one third of that in the Championship. Despite this there would be very few conversations of the 'they don't pay me enough' nature, which is standard practice in the football world despite being paid several times the UK's average wage. Most people find something to moan about, footballers are no different.

'Training' begins

I hadn't performed a run of note (longer than what I do on a match day as a warm up) since having the meniscus ligament in my knee removed as a 22 year old. The manager knew this, maybe he'd forgotten - day one and its 4 x 1000m runs.

We were given our training kit and I donned the sweatshirt for the first time: Fruit of the Loom with a Brentford FC badge sewn on. Only the best. It would soon be more use as a T-shirt after a few washes.

To say that my performance was embarrassing would be an understatement. I came last in every run, well actually goalkeeping coach Simon Royce joined me in that honour, although I'm sure he could have nudged ahead of me if he had chosen to. He stayed by my side for moral support, and I appreciated that. My knee did not appreciate the run.

I woke up the next day and as expected my knee was in no fit state to train as it was twice the size of the previous day. But, being day two at a new club, I was in no position to start pulling out of training. First impressions are important. On day two, it was running again, this time the bleep test. And I thought football had evolved.

I'm no strength and conditioning guru but I know the basics. It is commonly known that the way you train will affect muscle memory, and performance will mirror how you train. So, doing long same-paced runs won't increase power, it's great if you wish to burn fat or become a marathon runner but this isn't training for a goalkeeper.

If you were to consider a goalkeeper's game it wouldn't take a genius to understand what the key training points are. A goalkeeper will sprint maybe three or four times over 90 minutes, and for the majority of the match won't go any quicker than walking pace. What a goalkeeper may have to do however is make a point blank save or spring up into the top corner to tip away a drive – explosive power. A goalkeeper must train in this way in order to improve. If anything, long runs are detrimental to a goalkeeper's game, reinforcing slow twitch fibres and leading to a loss of explosiveness.

The manager knew my thoughts but they were falling on deaf ears. I called my dad that night 'Dad, I think I've made a mistake'. It's too late now.

Training improved slightly over the following week due to the fact that I spent some time with folks who would become my new goalkeeping fraternity. There was Simon Moore, a 20 year old lad scouted from the Isle of Wight, one of the nicest lads you could ever meet and incredibly talented, he may only be young but he would provide some stiff competition. And there was Simon Royce, who I had played against when he was at Gillingham. Simon was someone I was excited to work with. He had enjoyed an impressive career and although he was gradually moving into the coaching role he still showed glimpses in training of why he played at the top level. 'Happy go lucky' is how I'd describe Roycie and training with him and Si Moore would be the biggest positive to come out of the first couple of weeks. Roycie didn't officially have a coaching badge but he knew goalkeeping and could appreciate how a goalkeeper needs to work. We were on a similar wavelength, we hit it off instantly and I was confident he could get the best out of me.

A pre-season tour to Portugal was soon on the agenda, and rapidly followed by a game against Fulham. The Portugal trip went relatively smoothly other than being made to do a mammoth shooting session on hard ground. Little appreciation for goalkeepers, everyone taking pot shots with little rest time, this training wasn't even game related for the strikers. I wanted to take off my gloves and walk away from the training complex but this would do me no favours and would soon earn me a bad name although I'm sure my knee would have thanked me.

I was however aware my body language wasn't good. I knew I needed to reframe my thinking and *refocus* on what I was doing, but I continued under the hope that things would improve. With games on the agenda, I naturally assumed that training would be taken down a notch or two, so maybe this was the respite I had been looking for.

Power of body language

There are two key points to body language, the first one being that the simple action of smiling, sticking your chest out and breathing deeply will make you feel a whole lot better than if you were frowning, hunched over, and your breathing was shallow. Physiology will have a direct influence on your mindset. Secondly it will have an impact on the perceptions of others. Someone who adopts a powerful physiology is considered to be confident whereas I could sense my body language was the direct opposite of this. I didn't exude confidence, I wasn't happy, and I wasn't doing anything to change my state.

We returned from Portugal to face Fulham in our first friendly.

Let the games begin

I instantly took a liking to club captain Kevin O'Connor. David Hunt (Hunty) had always spoken very highly of Kev and I could instantly see why. Kev was very genuine in his ways and epitomised the label of 'model professional'.

Kev was in his testimonial year, and knowing that would give me the one bit of banter I could hold over Kev - that of his age! Technically he's only 6 months older than me but I soon established he would have been in the year above at school and I have since referred to him as a father figure. His ever increasing amount of grey flecks adding to the impression. It is now becoming rather tiresome banter, but age really is all I have on him! Kev's career to date has been a substantial one, he has accumulated well over 400 appearances for Brentford in 10 years and as a reward Fulham FC would be our first opponents (pre-season) for Kev's landmark game.

It had been a while since my last game in front of a crowd but that didn't change the standard emotions being present on a match day. I didn't understand these emotions at an earlier age but simply put, the emotion is fear. Fear of the unknown and an awareness that the body will soon be taken out of its comfort zone. Those who can control this fear can use it to take their game to new levels; those who get engulfed by it crumble, or 'choke' as it's often referred too.

I had prepared well. Other than fluid on my knee which the anti-inflammatory tablets would help settle, I felt good. I decided to drive to the ground early and get my own pre match meal in a hotel nearby. This was something I had been used to doing with Watford as it also helped ensure that I wouldn't be late for a game. Living in Watford meant that the journey was only twenty five minutes without traffic but I had already experienced a two hour trip home one day, courtesy of a stationary M25, and did not want to leave anything to chance.

The match actually started okay, although it was unusual being in a game situation again. It had been so long. I was also very aware how close the home crowd were behind me, and how loud they were. This may have been a friendly but the rivalry between Fulham and Brentford was there to be seen, a good opportunity to make an early impression, which I would do, just not a good one.

Mid-way through the first half I hooked a goal kick straight to one of Fulham's midfielders. Instantly I figured that as long as we made a tackle the kick would be forgotten. We didn't. They broke down our right, and cut the ball to the edge of the box for the shot. It was a tame shot to my right, I fell to my right to make a collapsing save only to feel the ball squirm under my hands and nestle in the net. I could hear the groans of the home fans; a long night was in store.

One became two, then three. I made a save at 3-0 which was accompanied by sarcastic cheers, 35 minutes into my debut and the crowd were turning on me already! We would go into half time 4-0 down and eventually lose 5-0. The Fulham fans chanted '5-0 and it's all your fault'. Technically I wasn't at fault for the remaining four goals but this didn't offer any comfort, this wasn't a good night.

How many have they scored, Rich?

What topped the night off was when I walked outside the ground to be greeted by an eager young fan who was collecting the autographs of all the players. He handed me his programme and pen and asked me who I was. 'I'm the goalkeeper,' I replied, as I went to scribble my name on his programme. At that point he snatched the programme and pen back and said 'Oh okay, no thank you'

Further setback

It was important for me to get back on track against our next opponents: Wycombe. Well, at least that was the plan until Roycie broke the news that Simon Moore would play against Wycombe and I'd play the following night against Staines Town. I was one game into my Brentford career, I certainly didn't need a rest... I had been dropped. Okay I thought, play well against Staines and get myself back on track. Or maybe not.

I am honest in that I have to say the Staines game was the worst game I have ever played. My kicking was appalling, I was at fault for two goals and I was very aware of the abuse I was getting from more than a handful of fans. I could sense them questioning me and I was questioning myself. I remember stopping on the way home with a thousand thoughts running around my head.

The main thought I had was of disappointment in myself. I hadn't given this game the desired mental focus it needed. I had prepared well physically, slept well and eaten the right things but I entered the game too relaxed. There needs to be 'tension', or at least *in my case* there does. We all have an 'Optimum Performance State', the best players are aware as to what their OPS is, and they lock into it week in week out. It's no surprise they get the desired results. Inconsistent players often haven't discovered their OPS and will allow game situations and confidence levels to control them as opposed to creating their own script. I knew this information, I just wasn't acting upon it and now I had self-confidence doubts and could feel myself heading down a destructive path.

What happened to the Richard Lee that had played so well in the Premiership a few years previously? I'm 27, surely I should now be in my prime?! Was I trying too hard to make an impression? Had two years on the bench changed me, why did I even want it anymore?! Perhaps I wasn't even that good when I was playing in the Premiership, I just had a couple of fortunate games and now I was getting exposed? I don't even like this game. I've never liked this game. Maybe I could become a coach, or a pundit? Yeah I like the idea of being a pundit, I could easily tell everyone else what they are doing wrong and that way I'd never be in the firing line myself.

Goals

Back to the drawing board and time to revisit the goals I had set myself for the season. I split my goals into 'outcome goals' and 'process goals'; basically this is the equivalent to the 'what' I wanted, and the 'how' I was going to get it.

Outcome goals included:

- Become player of the season at Brentford

- Be League One goalkeeper of the season

- Help Brentford to promotion

The Process goals were as follows:

- One hour gym work EVERYDAY

- Imagery training, 3 times per week

- Live in the present for games, intense focus.

It wasn't going to be easy achieving these goals if I wasn't in the team! And in truth it wasn't so much the goals that I had problems with, it was the 'why' that I was struggling with. I'm a huge believer that if given a big enough reason 'why' - then you'll find a way. I remember hearing the story of the woman who picked up a car in order to free her trapped son, something deemed impossible under normal circumstances but given enough of an incentive she found a way.

Another big motivation for a lot of lads I know is that of their kids. Not only do they want to make them proud but they want to offer them the best upbringing possible. With this in mind they have that extra added incentive to give everything in their power to succeed. I don't have any kids and I can't imagine that my performances are going to save anyone's life so I was going to have to keep thinking.

It wasn't that I didn't want to achieve my goals, I just couldn't think of a big enough reason for me to continue to give everything to a game that I felt had caused me so much pain, not only physically with my array of injuries, but emotionally over the years. Here I was, again, with criticism coming from all angles, questioning myself and wondering whether I had actually made the correct move in leaving the nice warm comfortable bench at Watford (where I had a certain status and respect having represented the club for such a long period of time) to this, which felt like the polar opposite. I knew what I needed to do in order to change my fortune. I needed to find that 'why' and along with it use renewed motivation to give everything to a game I had already given 19 years to. Despite knowing what I needed to do, I didn't act upon it, I was going through the motions.

I didn't play the next couple of pre-season games and I was pulled into the manager's office just before the final pre-season match. I was informed that I wasn't playing and that it was because I didn't appear to be enjoying it. It didn't take Sherlock Holmes to figure that one out, it was written all over me. I didn't want to be there and they didn't want me there. I had heard tales of recent keepers who were soon discarded and cast aside at Brentford. I looked odds on to join that list. In my defence I had been given two pre-season games despite not having played for a year, and I had expected a little more faith however badly I had played.

To give credit where it is due - Simon Moore had a fantastic pre-season. This lad's going to be a big name soon. I've worked with some of the best over the years and he's up there, technically spot on and physically made to be a goalkeeper. This didn't console me but if anyone were to play ahead of me then I was happy that it was him. Well for a short while at least.

The Ghost of Szczesny

One other thing I was made aware of - was the 'ghost' left behind by the previous Brentford keeper: Wojciech Szczesny, who was now fighting it out for a first team spot at Arsenal. I always remember the hole left when Peter Schmeichel left Manchester United; several tried to replace him – Barthez, Bosnich, Taibi and Howard – they were all fantastic keepers but Schmeichel cast a large shadow and arguably it wasn't until Edwin van der Sar joined United several years later that someone could claim that position as their own. Perhaps Brentford was not quite in the same league but I knew how fondly Griffin Park took to Szczesny and naturally comparisons would be made with whoever occupied the sticks. Another obstacle. One positive note was that July was out of the way. Surely the only way was up from here?

Blog I

Superstitions (June 2008)

It's Friday 13th June 08; heavy tropical thunderstorms in Orlando and I'm sat by the window of the Boeing plane from which we are about to take off.

The airport is drenched and the pilot comes on the speaker to announce it's a 50/50 chance as to whether we'd be taking off or not as he was unsure if we could beat the next storm in order to take off. The situation I and all the other passengers aboard our flight faced got me thinking about superstitions, where they originated and what affect they have had, and can have.

Firstly I wanted to know why Friday the 13th was thought to be unlucky, where could this have derived from, and my research pointed towards religion: the events of Good Friday, the day Jesus Christ was crucified, according to Christian lore, Adam and Eve also supposedly ate the forbidden fruit on a Friday 13th, the Great Flood started on this day, the builders of the Tower of Babel were tongue-tied and the Temple of Solomon was destroyed on a Friday the 13th. Coincidence? Or a real reason to be superstitious of this day?

There is also the notion that the mind will find reasons to back up any belief, so for instance if someone held the belief that

Friday the 13th was unlucky for them, they could go out of their way to find reasons as to why that's the case. Reasons that may well just be pure coincidences.

For me, a superstition of my past wasn't so much of Friday the 13th but just the number 13. After having a breakthrough season of sorts and playing my first senior games wearing the number 30 shirt, I began the next season in the number 13 shirt.

I then proceeded to twist my ankle, missing an England Under-21 call-up. I then endured getting concussed just a week before the beginning of the season and then a few weeks later split my upper arm in two, missing the majority of the season. Whose fault could this be?? Well the number of course!

I look back now and deem this a bit ridiculous (although I won't go out of my way to change back any time soon!). I wore number 16 the following season and finished the season breaking my cheekbone, rupturing my bicep and needing an operation on my knee but I never even questioned the number - why would I? 16 isn't thought to be unlucky!

Consciously I think we all know that superstitions don't make much sense but if the thought of them is having a positive effect on a performance or on your life then they are not necessarily wrong. However my personal thought is that superstitions can be very limiting, more mentally than anything.

What if a lifelong superstition couldn't be fulfilled, would everything you have built just collapse around you? Most of us with superstitions have, at some point, been forced to break them and, more times than not, the outcome has been fine. Quite often whatever happened would then take over and become the new superstition!

Superstitions are simply based around ones belief, they are often created in order to allow you to enter a frame of mind best suited for the situation you are about to face. Realistically, is there some mystical power attached to 'putting on your shirt when you come out of the tunnel' or those 'lucky pants'? Unlikely. What if you had the power to slip into that optimum frame of mind without the need for that superstition and weren't reliant on something which you can't always control?

The fact that I'm writing this means that obviously the flight was fine (despite some turbulence!) and we took off without delay... and for some unknown reason this flight wasn't particularly full, which meant I had two seats to myself!

I wonder why that could be???

3

August
Another Season
Another Bench

The full season began and we faced Carlisle away in our first game, and as expected I was warming the bench. This wasn't confirmed, however, until two hours before the game with the manager choosing the option of leaving everyone in uncertainty prior to each game. It was genuine uncertainty as we rarely worked on team shape prior to a game so no clues were offered up. Some speculated that, by naming the team so late, no one was given the opportunity to corner the manager in his office and ask the question 'why'.

Taking my place on the bench meant that the season was similar to many previous seasons, other than that the stadiums weren't quite as vast, and rather than the big bucket seats that many of the Premiership and Championship teams now have, it was, as the word suggested, a bench. We lost the opening game 2-0.

Three days later, though, we won in the first round of the Carling Cup. I was delighted for Simon Moore as he put in very capable performances in both games - if he was to continue the form he was showing I could have no complaints. However, that particular night I *would be* given reason for complaint and Simon more so.

While browsing the internet I naturally had a quick look on the club's website to see if there was any news of note. The site informed me that we'd signed goalkeeper Alex McCarthy on loan. A heads up would have been nice.

I drove to training the next morning and continued my usual routine of stopping at McDonald's to get my porridge and cappuccino. A little ritual I have is to instantly peel off the sticker on the cappuccino and stick it on the loyalty card, ensuring that I don't go over any lines I shouldn't. It brings back memories of collecting football stickers as a child.

I'll never forget one Christmas in particular when my dad told me that Santa had brought me an entire box of stickers, and this meant 100+ packs of stickers. At that age I was very impressed that my dad had been in regular contact with Santa and ensured that he knew to head down the football route with regards to presents. I was so excited. I couldn't sleep at all and woke my parents up at the earliest opportunity (at least technically classed as Christmas day). The stickers would accompany a spherical shaped present which left little to the imagination but made me immensely happy. Maybe I once loved football? I certainly knew every statistic on every top flight player at that time, and could recite the 1989 "Race for the Championship" VHS off by heart, and my particular favourite 'Saves Galore'.

Meeting No2

Cappuccino in hand, I entered the manager's office first thing. I always arrived earlier than everyone else and judging from the manager's body language he was visibly taken aback upon seeing me. He perked up a bit when his assistant Terry Bullivant joined him.

I had known Terry or 'Bully' as he was commonly known in the football world from my time at Watford when he was the assistant to Ray Lewington. It was the season that I made my breakthrough at Watford as a 22 year old, a season that I had started well by helping Watford reach a semi-final of the League Cup. For the semi, a two legged game against Liverpool awaited, before a broken cheek bone and eye socket injury would cost me what promised to be the biggest game of my life. I did return later that season but couldn't recreate my early season form, not helped by a ruptured bicep and torn knee cartilage.

I liked Bully. His presence was, in the main, for the bubbly atmosphere he helped create around the place, and my guess is that he was the main instigator behind my move to Griffin Park. He wouldn't say anything in this meeting though.

I explained my disappointment at finding myself third choice keeper at such an early stage of the season. I may not have been enjoying myself but I was still applying myself in training and my career suggested that I was worth a chance at this level at least. The manager's reply seemed odd to me: "you are not our third choice goalkeeper, you are our number one goalkeeper. You're just not playing at the moment." I found his comment patronising. I then asked the big question: "do you want me here?" His reply? "It's up to you if you stay, however if you want to go we won't stand in your way". This angered me.

Chapter 3 - August

'A setback is a setup for a comeback'

Earlier in life, the natural thing I would have done would have been to blame the manager for the situation I found myself in. I'm sure I would have received plenty of sympathy from friends and family in doing so but what good would it have done me? In truth no one cares. Who cares what you *could've, should've, might've* been? People close to you will try to be nice and sympathise with you but does this change anything? Setbacks happen all the time. So what if the manager has dropped me and treated me the way he has? I wonder... if I complain to enough people whether he'll tell the world how sorry he is and beg for my forgiveness? It all comes down to responsibility; things won't always be fair or right, it's not about what has happened, it's about finding a way to bounce back from each setback. Be clear in your goal, know why you are after it, then find a way to do it, or make one. It's as simple as that.

In an odd twist, on the back of all this, I kept my place on the bench ahead of Si Moore. Si had been demoted to third choice. How bizarre and what a bad message to send out - although I could understand it in that it would certainly keep me quiet for a short while.

Things didn't go well for Alex. We took one point from four games and a few costly mistakes meant he would leave after a month. Similarly to me, and judging from the discussions we had, I know this experience made him appreciate what he had. He didn't have to stay and he didn't want to. Having worked with him I could see what an impressive talent he was, which he would prove later in the season when selected for both Reading and impressing with the England Under-21 team.

Alex's departure meant a glimmer of hope for me, and during this time an opportunity presented itself in a cup game against Hull. I wouldn't find out until we met for the match whether I would play or not, but I had a feeling this would be an opportunity. Without sounding overdramatic, and aware the season was still young, this was perhaps my last opportunity.

A reason why

A belief I hold is that if you have a big enough reason 'why' then you'll find a way to succeed in what you are trying. I often hear extraordinary stories of people going above and beyond conceivable thinking when given a big enough reason why.

I saw a documentary recently of a blind man who had learned to use a form of sonar hearing, similar to that of a bat, in order to ride a bike like someone with full vision. He would make a clicking noise as he rode and would listen for the smallest echo to decipher his surroundings. By not having vision he dedicated his time to heightening other senses with his goal of being able to lead a fantastic life despite what many would consider a major setback. He certainly had a powerful reason why. We hear of miraculous examples regularly and I have no doubt each situation comes with its own powerful incentive to go above and beyond what is considered possible.

I had a strange but powerful 'why' as a teenager and I've no doubt it helped push me to acquire the skills I have today. And it had nothing to do with 'the love of the game'.

Firstly, I must mention that I wasn't the most confident kid, far from it, especially when it came to talking to girls. At the age of 11 I managed to go out with a girl I had always liked called Kelly. Now Kelly was known for kissing boys behind the swimming pool at the school on lunch breaks. Despite being hugely tempted by the chance to experience my first kiss I chickened out and instead opted to join the rest of my friends in playing football for the entire lunch break. The 'relationship' lasted three days.

Later, when I started secondary school, I would fall for someone on my very first day. Sitting at the front of the coach (the older kids at the back) I was one of the first pick up points. A few miles into our journey we stopped in Great Kimble and a tall slim blonde girl walked onto the coach. Her name was Charlotte Stevenson, I was besotted – *she* was my reason why.

My thought process went a little something like this: I had decided that by becoming a professional footballer I would have the chance to be with Charlotte. Footballers get all the girls right? Such a simple idea was a hugely powerful one to me at that time. I would get home every evening, and take my football into the lounge where I had set up my own training centre! This mainly consisted of a sofa that I could roll the ball against. Thanks to the ridge at the bottom, the ball would pop up around chest height allowing me to catch it using the 'W' technique. The lounge also had a beam which was ideal for practicing my cross taking! I would practice for hours, a variety of techniques needed to improve with one simple thought behind it all – Charlotte. I now realise there is no right or wrong 'why' as long as it's powerful enough.

Back at Brentford, it was now or never, and this became my 'why'. The thought of 'what if I don't succeed at Brentford?' was driving me forwards.

In my learning I came across an idea which has really stuck with me. It relates to pain and pleasure, more precisely how the majority of us would rather focus on the avoidance of pain than the pursuit of pleasure gain. The most common example would be that of an unhappy relationship with neither person willing to make the decision that needs to be made for the promise of a brighter future elsewhere. This is often due to fear of the unknown or the initial pain that would be endured in actually breaking up. What generally happens is that the relationship gradually reaches a tipping point, at which point it becomes more painful to remain with that person than not. This is when the relationship ends. Right now, before I could even think about the pursuit of pleasure, I needed to avoid the pain of failure.

A different reality hit me. Which club would take me if I was discarded? I hadn't played in years and should Brentford get rid of me after two months, would I get another league club? It's unlikely I would get one in the vicinity of where I live; I'd probably have to move. Also the money would never match what I was earning at Brentford, and it would be a far cry from what I was earning in the Premier League with Watford. And what would happen if I failed at any post-Brentford club too? Would my biggest achievement in football be that of appearing in an FA Cup semi-final which in truth I only played because Ben Foster was cup tied (he was contracted with Manchester United).

I didn't have a *positive* 'why', but I had a *powerful* 'why'. It would do for now.

Reframe and refocus

Time to reframe and refocus. I had a reason, now, to make it happen. No excuses, no blame games, stop being a victim. Just give everything to this game of football and accept the outcome. The script for me was simple, it's only possible to have control over certain elements, a win can never be guaranteed but you can give yourself the best possible chance.

'If nothing changes… nothing changes.'

What I was doing wasn't working. I needed to do something to get my edge back. I remembered back to a few years ago when, playing some of my best football, I would fall asleep listening to a Paul McKenna 'self-confidence' CD. It was habitual. Before I drifted off, I would press play and fall asleep hoping that whatever was said would sink into my subliminal mind and aid my performance. I was going through a good spell in my career so never questioned this at the time although for whatever reason I broke the habit and no longer know where that CD is.

Chapter 3 - August

I did wonder whether the CD had an impact though. I was playing very well and from memory I was confident at that time (as the CD's intention stated)! Hypnotism certainly couldn't hurt and what did I have to lose? I was already hovering above rock bottom.

In order to find the best hypnotist for me I would first need to do some thorough research. Or maybe I could just Google 'Watford hypnotist'? First result – 'exuberance hypno' with a Mr Dave Sabat. Perfect! Being the shrewd businessman that I claim to be I wrote to Dave offering the deal of a lifetime, some free hypnotherapy in exchange for some press coverage if he was able to help resurrect my floundering career. As luck would have it Dave was a big Watford fan, knew who I was, and felt he could be the answer to my self-doubts. A deal was made and it would work out to be the best business deal I would do all year. It wouldn't work out too badly for Dave either.

Meeting Dave

I will speak in this book about four mentors that were instrumental for me over the season and despite only meeting Dave in August he would play a pivotal role in the course of my season. It can be quite rare to meet someone who you instantly know is on a similar wavelength to yourself but this is what I had with Dave. He welcomed me into his clinic and the first thing that struck me was the speed at which he spoke. I'm aware that speed and tone of voice play a large role in gaining rapport with someone, the idea being that you can adapt your speech to match that of someone you feel it important to gain rapport with. The logic behind this being that *people like people like themselves*.

I'm also a quick talker naturally so we spent the first half an hour discussing football and it was clear that many of our ideas on performance matched. I explained that I had a lot of knowledge of the mind, my issue was more in implementing the theory and putting it into practice. Dave's confidence in his ability shone through instantly, he believed in his capabilities, I knew I was in safe hands.

I explained my thoughts at that time. I was uninspired with football and was seriously reconsidering what I wanted to do. The thought of a new challenge did inspire me but I knew that if there was a way I could enjoy the game of football this would win over any other options. That was why I sat in his chair preparing to be hypnotised. Dave didn't even consider my suggestion of a different pursuit, he told me that football was my calling and that the best was yet to come. I didn't believe him at that time but I wanted to believe him so I put my trust in him and allowed myself to fall into a hypnotic state. I soaked up all the positive ideas he presented.

Hull City – a new beginning

As well as being hypnotised I also made other changes. Rather than wearing my tired looking black Umbro boots I bought some white Adidas Predators along with white socks. I also asked that rather than wearing extra-large kit that I wear a much tighter fitting large keeper's shirt. Next on the list was a haircut. This is quite a common one; often when people want to elicit change a haircut is the way forward - David Beckham being the most noteworthy example of this, and why not, it certainly can't hurt. In the grand scheme of things these may seem insignificant and it is a form of 'taking control', but there is also the belief that if you look good then you'll feel good.

The problem I now face when getting my hair trimmed, though, is that it's not so much a case of having it cut into a certain style as much as having the thicker areas cut in such a way as to match in with the areas that are now thinning at a rapid rate. The style is the least of my worries! With each cut it's turning more and more into a precise operation, removing hair follicles individually in an attempt to fight baldness for another week. I have actually had the implant procedure made famous by Wayne Rooney on my head, implanting hair into barren areas, although this was primarily on the front of my hairline. The issues I have at 27 are very much around the crown area. The end of any haircut, when I'm offered the mirror from behind to check out the back of my head, used to be an irrelevance. I now anticipate it with anxiety, always curious as to whether I will soon be sporting a Pepe Reina style or returning for further surgery on the crown area!

I guess it's a good job I own a hat business.

Back to Hull

Of all the teams we were due to face (on what was a crucial day personally) it had to be Hull City. Hull City was the team who had cost me and Watford FC a shot at the Premier League a few years earlier in what was perhaps my lowest moment as a footballer (more about this later). Could I settle a personal score with them or would they consign me to further distress?

Game day arrived. Despite the work on the mind I had done over the past few days I was still nervous. In fact very nervous. I knew the enormity of this match. A bad game and I could be another 'Lewis Price' never to be seen in a Brentford shirt again.

We conceded early, no one said it would be straightforward.

I had made a promise to myself at the start of the season that individual incidents are irrelevant, focus for 90 minutes and analyse your performance after the game, so I reminded myself of this: focus, focus, focus. Although generally well controlled I still had the odd fruitless thought pop into my head, one being that it is a fact that when a team goes behind they stand (on average) less than a 10% chance of winning that particular game. This may not apply to the likes of Manchester United if they were to go one behind but it did apply to Brentford conceding first against Hull. The odds were against us.

A wand of a left foot.
And all it took was a pair of white Predators!

I made a couple of decent stops in the first half before Robbie Simpson fired a fantastic free kick into the top corner to draw us level at the break. I walked in at half time pleased, I had rediscovered how to strike a football and I had a feeling of confidence once more. I continued this throughout the second half making a full length save from a free kick. I felt a surge of energy rush through me, something I hadn't felt in a while but in that moment, that instance, I had a reminder of what football can offer. I was aware of the applause from around me, but knew I needed to refocus quickly.

Five minutes were left in the match and a pinpoint Brentford delivery was met by the onrushing Marcus Bean to head home what would turn out to be a dramatic winner. There was one more dramatic situation of my own to go through, and one that I consider to be quite pivotal in hindsight. It would come in the

Chapter 3 - August

final minute, a free kick struck from 25 yards which I decided to parry rather than catch, it wasn't a particularly tough free kick and I should have caught it. The ball rebounded against their striker only to fall kindly in front of me to scoop up. A bit of luck at last. I like the thought that *you create your own luck* and I was certainly due some. I'd live to fight another day.

4

September
Toffee Treats

My next opportunity to impress would come against Stevenage
in the cup. As mentioned in the last chapter, Alex McCarthy
hadn't had a particularly great time during his loan spell at
Brentford, and we were now in the relegation zone. I knew a
good performance here and I'd be back on track and a chance to
cement my place could come my way. I guess, given the start I'd
had, I should have expected more drama.

Red mist

As I sat in the changing room, ready to warm up, Mickey Spillane
leant over and informed me that another goalkeeper, Ben
Hamer, had joined us on loan from Reading. I'm sure Mickey
didn't mean any harm by this and I think he assumed I was
aware. I wasn't.

Chapter 4 - September

I was literally on my way out of the door to warm up when he told me, and my head began to spin. Surely Mickey was misinformed? I asked Roycie if it was true and I could instantly tell Mickey was spot on. Roycie was in a tough position; he knew it would do me no favours to tell me this information just before a game - but he confirmed that it was true. I was seething, the manager has done it again I thought. This time, rather than Sky Sports News informing me, it was one of my team mates.

Seeing red I walked back into the changing room. "Boss, can I have a word?" I asked. He made me wait a short while as he put the set pieces on the wall. At this particular moment I despised him, his arrogance, but I remained as calm as I could. Finally he joined me away from the squad. "We've signed Ben Hamer," I said to him. It was more of a statement than a question but I wanted some reason, some explanation. Yes, you are the manager, you have tough decisions to make but surely there is room for some common decency?! I had done everything and more asked of me, I made a huge commitment in leaving Watford on the back of our discussion pre-season and you treat me like this? The answer was short and sweet. "Yes." That was it, nothing more. He even had the audacity to look shocked that I was angry with this situation. In fact angry is an understatement, I was livid.

We exchanged a few words before he loudly said that I didn't have to play if I didn't want to. I called him something that I shouldn't have done, and under different circumstances it may well have got me the sack before I walked out onto the pitch. I may have been walking out onto the pitch but this didn't mean I was definitely going to play.

My dad was in the crowd so I went and explained what had just happened. I was 50/50 as to what to do; part of me wanted to go home but this was against my nature. This had nothing to do with him, this was for me. Decision made - I decided to play.

I started the game well making a good save to my top left. The vibe I got from the Brentford fans was beginning to shift, I heard the song "you used to be shite but now you are alright!" It made me smile.

We scored. Robbie Simpson who had started the season on fire (a fantastic acquisition from Huddersfield on loan) slotted home. I pushed a couple of kicks late in the first 45, but all in all a solid half.

We were trying to play an attractive style of football but not all that successfully. This was very much the script for the season. Brentford had gained a reputation for playing a very direct style of football in the previous couple of seasons, which in truth had brought success. But with improvements in other teams, as well as an increased budget, the club now felt this was no longer acceptable. The board and supporters demanded attractive football, in order to get out of this league we would need to play our way out. This certainly increased the pressure on the manager and we looked like a team caught somewhere in the middle. It wasn't good to watch. It did however mean that I would have plenty to do once again in the second half.

It was clear during this game that the boss was losing patience with trying to play the ball around without success; on the whole results were very poor, and we would soon revert back to what we'd done previously.

'If you look for something hard enough you will find it.'

There is a belief, held by some, that you find what you want to find. This is true in life and in football. This seemed to be true in that every time we'd play a long ball behind a defence that forced a defender to lose possession - this would be highlighted as a positive. On the flip side, it would be a negative if a player was to lose a ball attempting to play a pass that cost us possession in a dangerous area, as if to cement the idea that a direct style of football is the way to play the game. I didn't particularly like it as a keeper but it certainly simplified my game, bypass defence and midfield and hit the front man with every distribution.

What this meant was that the defenders were always favourites to win any ball I punted forward, I couldn't control whether we kept possession or not and therefore my stats would always reflect distribution poorly. My goal was therefore to keep hitting good areas - this was all I could control.

In a similar vein, this is why it can be so hard for a player to lose a tag that he may have gained. One that I certainly had at Watford was a criticism about my (in)ability to kick a ball; I knew I could kick a ball and do it well but when labelled as a poor kicker it soon became a belief that I adopted, knowing no different at the time. Managers would highlight the one or two wayward kicks I would offer in a match and I would get the odd groan from supporters when off target. Although keepers who were considered good kickers would hit a few wayward kicks, they would be labelled as 'uncharacteristic'. If someone wants to find something they will find it, and also find evidence to back it up.

The second half would be a good one for me, several sharp stops and a confident take to finish the game, one nil, another win. Expect to see me in the morning gaffer.

Another solid performance under my belt.

Cappuccino in hand

"One question. Am I playing Saturday?" I sat in the manager's office (again), Bully was also present. "I haven't made up my mind yet," came the response.

Hmmm, sure you haven't, I thought.

I had information telling me otherwise; Ben wasn't leaving the bench at Reading to warm a bench at Brentford. At this point I was given the option to leave again if I wanted to. My ego was telling me to leave, go somewhere I was appreciated even if it did mean a drop in level. But there was one big reason to stick around. Everton. We had drawn the Premiership giants after beating Hull in the cup. Ben was cup tied, I could consider my options after this game.

I know of many an example where a player joins a club only to be cast aside early on. The general result of this will be that the player either gets moved on and subsidised for any financial loss, or quite simply he gets his contract paid up. This idea has always baffled me, it seems apparent that in many instances you get rewarded for failing. However I could now appreciate how these players felt - when wronged you want justice of some kind.

It was also now apparent that I was among a rather large group who had been alienated, players who were similarly drafted in and soon to be cast aside. New face after new face arrived and players left at a similar rate. I however remained, sticking to my vow that I would follow the process I had set myself. Also, in truth, I knew that if I was to move from Brentford I would realistically be looking at League 2 and I was confident that I'm too good for that.

The season clearly wasn't going to plan but this certainly wasn't the first setback I had experienced in my career or my business life for that matter, and something I knew to be vitally important right now was that of flexibility in my approach.

Flexibility in approach – www.DrCap.co.uk

I met Daren soon after leaving secondary school, when I started life as an apprentice footballer at Watford FC. How we met was, in some ways, strange. I left Aylesbury Grammar school after completing my GCSEs at the time he joined to complete his A levels. I always say we met at school but this is somewhat inaccurate. However we did meet through mutual friends and it soon became apparent that we were like-minded in many of our ways, and it wasn't long before we became business partners.

When Daren and I conjured up our big plans on how our headwear company was going to take over the world we had a certain business plan in mind. Long story short it was based around a large number of retail outlets, each with high stock levels, regular new stock and a regular rotation of the stock to keep it fresh and ensure that each time a customer walked through the door they'd soon be wowed by our selection.

To begin with we opened a cart in the main shopping centre in Leicester selling a selection of New Era fitted caps. This was a success so we soon opened a shop nearby in Leicester and the business got off to a flyer. Word was spreading about our shop and takings were high. It was soon after we opened our shop that we appeared on Dragon's Den to explain our idea and how extra investment would mean that we could speed up the process. In the end, we secured £150,000 for a 50% equity stake in our business.

The investment never actually materialised after the show had aired but it didn't change anything. We still had the same plans, and it was simply the case that things would take a bit longer without the investment. As it turned out it would take a lot longer. Sales started to dip and we were beginning to see the full extent of the recession as our weekly takings dropped to a mere 20% of what we were drawing in the early days. For a while we continued to plug away with the hope that it would turn around again but it wasn't happening and we knew it.

We had plenty of stock, which we owned outright but the income was barely covering staff wages, let alone rental costs, and the money needed to buy new stock. For a while we had toyed with the idea of running a website in conjunction with the shop but we didn't have any money, especially the amount of money needed to build a website of this magnitude.

Impakt media, a company who had produced my personal website (www.richardleegk.com) were keen to make a Dr Cap website and we were keen for them to make the site too - the problem was simply that we couldn't afford them. Remembering a favourite quote of mine 'find a way or make one' we discussed different ideas before agreeing on a deal where the website would be built for free in exchange for a small percentage in the company going to Impakt media and a set percentage of all income. This worked for both parties, Impakt media had an incentive where, if they could make this site big, they could stand to earn a substantial amount of money. From our point of view this was a lifeline. We were floundering but the deal offered hope for what was such a promising start.

Soon afterwards, we closed the shop. We still had rent to pay for a couple more years but we knew it was time to cut our losses. At the time we considered this a failure but in hindsight it was anything but a failure.

'There is no such thing as failure, only feedback.'

What we were doing with Dr Cap wasn't working, therefore we needed a change in approach. With the website we had a change in approach, it was now time to let this take centre stage and focus our efforts on building this online direction rather than allowing the company to haemorrhage money via our shop.

Now, only a matter of a couple of years later the website is thriving, weekly takings are more than treble what we were getting in the shop at our peak, and all without the costs that come from leasing a retail outlet. We are now arguably the largest independent online headwear retailer in the UK, mainly thanks to the great work of Impakt media but the lesson for me was that of flexibility.

To begin with we never intended for Dr Cap to be an online-only business but had we not made the transition when we did then Dr Cap would now be bankrupt. I have no doubt. 'Roll with the punches,' as I've been told several times before. This saying holds a lot of truth - things don't always go as planned. Have an end outcome in mind, yes, but stubbornness and the rejection of available (unplanned) avenues could be costly.

Back in the football world, and as expected, Ben started Saturday's game, and I went public with my grievances. I was careful with what I said but I wanted it to be known that I hadn't come to Brentford to sit on a bench. I could have done that at a higher level on more money.

Credit where it's due. Ben performed admirably in his first 3 games, his side volley was majestic and I liked his style of goalkeeping, we began to climb the table steadily although scoring was still an issue.

Something else that didn't help my cause was that this wasn't Ben's first stint at Griffin Park. In fact it wasn't his second or third, but fourth! The last of which finished with a promotion. He was a favourite at Brentford, he would be tough to oust. I would, however, put this to the back of my mind. I couldn't control this. I could give a show against Everton, which was now upon us.

Better than Sex?

This game comfortably goes down as the best night of my life although the day leading to it was somewhat manic.

I had ordered some gloves for the game from my sponsor 'Sells'. The gloves hadn't arrived and it was game day. I had a worn pair that maybe had one game left (at best) but nothing else. As a goalkeeper having confidence in your gloves is huge, at pro level playing a game with gloves that lack grip is unacceptable, they simply are the tools of our trade.

I had to do something. I rushed to KeepersKit's warehouse on the morning of the game. They didn't stock the Sells brand due to a recent move from Sells that gave exclusivity to ProDirect. Not ideal. I know Adam Sells personally and he has looked after me for 10 years; I'd hate to have a good game and get pictured in a different brand but playing a bad game due to the gloves letting me down would be bad publicity for Adam!

Chapter 4 - September

I bought a different brand but these would be my back up. I called Adam and explained my predicament. Adam arranged for a friend of his to meet me personally prior to the game to provide me with a brand new pair. Problem averted. I arrived at the game to see a package sat on my place with two brand new pairs of Sells gloves! I didn't have a pair earlier that day and now I had several pairs! And after all the efforts exerted I decide to wear the ones I already had, but at least I was sure.

So the game begins, and we are one down within 5 minutes. The 'less than 10% stat' pops into my head again; in fact against Everton it's probably closer to 2%. This could be a long night, I reckon. I was helpless to save the goal and credit where it's due - it was a good finish into my top right hand corner. *Focus, focus, focus*, control what I can control. A few minutes later Yakubu slips through, I come off my line quickly to make a smothering save. I make several more contributions to keep it to one: a save mid-height to my right that was put behind, and a low save to my left. I feel good, at one with the game, my focus was pure.

With half time approaching we secured an equaliser - a fantastic header from Gaz Alexander – and we're back in this game. The atmosphere heats up. Half time, one each, so far so good.

Half time for me meant a pep talk from Roycie and out we go. In much the same vein as the first half I'm busy. I deny Yakubu again, Arteta from range and a double save on full time. Added to this we squander a chance to win it: Charlie McDonald sees his penalty saved. End of normal time, 1-1, what an achievement. Everton want this, their big guns are on.

We negotiate the first half of extra time safely, I make my way to our home fans for the start of the second period of extra time. They greet me generously. The Fulham memories are beginning to fade. Full time, penalties, I love penalties.

People always say to me: "penalties must be so nerve racking". Honestly? Not at all. This is as big an opportunity I get - to be a hero for a night.

In a similar fashion to the Hull game I had partaken in hypnotherapy the night before and quite curiously Dave had made a suggestion for saving a hypothetical Jermaine Beckford penalty. Why Beckford I am unsure, but this was in my mind as he approached.

The standard of penalties was high. I dived the correct way for the first two but both evaded me. I felt a moment of frustration when the third one went in. I didn't just play the game of my life for it to be forgotten in a shoot-out 'nearly' story. Thankfully our boys were showing great composure so the score was still level. Beckford stepped up. As he approached, the thought of the discussion with Dave entered my head, only briefly though. C'mon, this is the one I thought. He looked nervy. I could sense he had yet to win over the Everton faithful, this was no time for showing mercy though.

He stepped up and fired low to my left. I had dived mid height. I flung my arm down and felt the ball thud against my wrist and out to safety. YES! I felt the roar from behind me - it's amazing how much noise 8,000 people can make! Pure ecstasy, I felt the adrenalin course through my veins. Better than sex? Most definitely.

A special moment.

The rush!

But the game wasn't over. We scored our next penalty and with the score at 4-3 there was one penalty remaining for both teams. Phil Jagielka was last to take a penalty for Everton. I know Jags from my time as an England Under-18 international, and at the time (at that level) we were very much on the fringe of things. Jags has certainly gone on to big things, such a nice lad too, and although we had exchanged a few words beforehand it was all irrelevant right now. He looked pretty confident as he approached but then he always does. Will he smash it? If so then I'll stand still but I think he's got too much about him to just thump it. He's a player, he'll look to slot it. Left or right? I always make my decision as the ball is placed and then I stick with it and commit to it. He places the ball, need to make a decision… left, I'm going to dive left. He steps up, fires to my left, I'm at full stretch but it's out of my reach, I hear a noise, it's hit the post!

The next moments are a blur. I'm running but I'm not exactly sure where. There are hundreds of people on the pitch and I soon find myself back in the changing room. We were going crazy, what a night!

All he wanted was a cuddle.

I collected the man of the match trophy, and decided to go back to my parents to share a few glasses of red wine, and reply to the hundreds of texts, tweets, and emails I had received. It's not that often a night like this comes around. I knew it needed to be savoured.

A meal for two at the Radisson!

I barely slept that night. I don't normally read newspapers but I wanted to see what coverage we had received. I'd made all the back pages, I'm definitely back I figured! In the process I'd also stumbled across a new 'why'. I needed to prove that this manager was wrong to discard me.

Although the FA Cup semi-final, and the game away to Manchester United, may go down as bigger footballing occasions they certainly didn't match the Everton game for the high that I felt afterwards; this was comfortably my new number one football highlight. If only there were a way in which I could lock this feeling in, and experience it again and again...

Anchoring states

A simple definition of an anchor is experiencing a specific response when met with a certain stimulus. One of the simplest naturally occurring anchors is that of a song that takes you back and you instantly generate feelings associated with that song. For example, if I hear 'photograph' by Nickelback I'm instantly taken back to the sunshine skywalk bridge in Tampa Bay. I can picture the blue sea, the sun reflecting off it, and the warmth of the Floridian sun. It's coupled with a feeling of utter contentment and relaxation. This 'anchor' occurred naturally for me but there are ways in which we can create anchors and this has become a very powerful tool for me personally.

During a game I want to feel calm but alert, powerful but not tense. I wouldn't want to fire up my skywalk bridge anchor as this would be too relaxed for what I consider to be my personal Optimal Performance State. I therefore work on eliciting states outside of the game arena. I will recall different scenarios that have happened in the past that can help get me to the state I need to be in.

When I experience that state it's now essential I lock it in, never to be forgotten. The way I do this is through a specific movement allied to several keywords. My movement is quite a common movement, I press my middle finger against my thumb while repeating to myself *connect, connect, connect*. As bizarre as it may sound I soon find myself entering my OPS and the more often I do this the quicker it happens. This is a key tool for me, to know that in any game situation I can now lock into this state within a matter of seconds and give myself the best possible chance of performing well.

With the Everton memory lodged securely in the memory bank, surely I would now make my first league appearance?

Blog II

In Awe (July 2008)

I, like millions of others, sat back on Sunday evening and watched two of the best tennis players ever to have graced this planet fight it out to be crowned Wimbledon champion: Roger Federer and Rafael Nadal.

The game itself was immense and I personally got more from watching that than anything for a long time.

The intensity of the two players was there to be seen; both seemed incredibly calm under the severest of pressure. They were a fine example to sports men and women around the world. By watching, I got the impression that it was almost irrelevant as to what the score was, they just seemed to play each point on its merit with very little care or regard as to whether a mistake would mean a game lost. What I guess I'm trying to say is that they gave the impression that they were playing without fear.

For anyone who's played tennis they'll understand what I mean when I say that you adapt your game to the circumstances you are faced with. For instance, if you're 30-40 down then it's vital you keep the ball in court, for fear that one mistake and the game is over. It can be common to cramp up and not play the way you want to play.

Chapter 4 - September

This seemed to matter little during this match. On a few occasions, Federer had 'championship point' against him and he just continued to try and make shots without much regard for the situation he faced - and the same could be said for the eventual winner Rafael Nadal.

I then thought of the idea of applying this to all sports: football for instance. Many a time a team goes one-nil up and then decides to sit back and invite pressure. I understand that many tactics come into play but there can be a shift of thought from the idea that 'we want to score a goal' to 'we want to protect what we have'. This can be a dangerous thought as it will often mean that the team in front will have little in terms of attacking power and are vulnerable to a mistake or good play from the opposition that may result in an equaliser.

What if a team decided that they would pay no attention to the score and just play the game for 90-plus minutes and continue to do as many positive things as they could for that time, whether they were 5-0 up or 5-0 down? Or even look at the bigger picture and commit to this over a season? A team so in tune with their state that they ensured that all 11 players played each and every game with confidence at a peak.

Golf could be another example. Why is Tiger Woods so much better than the rest? (As of writing this!) Why does he always perform well under pressure? My belief is that thanks to plenty of mental training, he now has the ability to clear all else from his mind except the desired outcome he wants. His focus is purely on what he is after, not what he wants to avoid.

For instance, he is faced with a Par 3, water to the left, bunker to the right and out of bounds over the back of the green. I believe these thoughts wouldn't enter his head; it would simply be a case of where the flag is and how close he can get to it. Positive thinking without fear is a great combination and one that many successful people have in common.

It was somewhat sad that someone had to lose the Wimbledon final because in truth there was very little between the two competitors and, right to the end, both showed class.

In the post-match interviews, Federer was gracious in defeat and Nadal heaped praise on Federer, saying that he'd beaten the best of all-time. No hate, just appreciation for each other and the situation they both find themselves in. I have no doubt this will do little to diminish the path that Federer finds himself on, if anything he'll use it in such a way to motivate himself further.

For me it was fantastic entertainment and a fine example to all involved in sport.

5

October
The Road to Recovery
can be Long

The manager had another big decision to make, or at least it should have been a big decision. I had just played the game of my life, I was on fire, and my hunger for the game had returned. Was I beginning to enjoy this? In fairness to Ben he'd enjoyed a very solid start - three clean sheets in a row and barely put a foot wrong. We were in a peculiar situation.

Two first choice goalkeepers

The gaffer had said for some time that he wanted two number ones, but I still needed this explaining to me, and also for someone to give me an example where this idea had been successful. Even the sentence itself made me laugh when he told me "two number ones". I thought he was joking. He wasn't. Ben texted me after the Everton game - "Incredible tonight mate, honestly don't know why I'm here" it read. I had no issues with Ben, in fact we struck up a good friendship early on; he simply wanted to play first team football and with limited opportunities at Reading, a move to Brentford was a good one.

With regard to the 'two number ones' idea, there are several reasons why this has never been successful in the goalkeeping world. Firstly, playing in goal is very different to playing outfield. We rarely get fatigued in games so tiredness should never be an issue. Secondly, and generally speaking, goalkeepers get better as the number of games increase. It is thanks to match experience that you are usually able to read the game that bit better, hence it is believed most keepers peak in their thirties. To swap keepers on a regular basis will mean that rhythm is hard to come by; to play a game cold is tough, you can train all day long, and work on technique, but the experience of match situations, decision making, positioning, etc is best honed in games.

Something else that has always been apparent to me is that the best goalkeepers have always had the backing of the manager. Peter Schmeichel famously had some rough spells - but was he ever dropped? No, the reason being that Alex Ferguson knew that he was a fantastic goalkeeper and that form is only temporary. In the goalkeeping world (and this applies to the outfield also) uncertainty leads to insecurity which in turn leads to inconsistency. I was playing the highest standard of football I had ever played yet hadn't started a league game and three other keepers had. I was fully aware that I was at a critical crossroads in my career, and each game took on an extra emphasis. Despite the performances against Hull, Stevenage, and Everton I was still a bad game away from the goalkeeping graveyard. "Oh yeah I remember Richard Lee, never quite cut it at Watford, I think he went to Brentford after that, or was it Bradford?!" - no one wants to be *that* guy.

When entering the football world, like many other humans on this planet, we strive for significance. A basic human need, as a footballer, means reaching the top, being admired, respected and held in high esteem, not another 'also ran'. I'm 28 but still harbour those dreams, I have to, but I'm back up in League One right now. No excuses. Onwards and upwards, and demand high standards.

Ben started the next game as expected; my next challenge would come in the Johnstone's Paint Trophy several weeks later, against Leyton Orient.

JPT

Approaching the Leyton Orient game - we were in poor form, once again lingering around the relegation zone and our performances deserved exactly that. Would the cup bring the best out of us? No, it was a dreadful game. It was a 7pm kick off, and as with all JPT games, the crowd barely topped 500. The standard of football was horrific for two teams playing at League One level. I was playing the game and if it weren't for the constant self-talk I find myself doing every game I would have been incredibly bored. I would often break out into song when the ball was out of play and up the other end, something I do when needing a break from intense concentration. It would generally be the last song I had listened to before crossing the white line, and that day's choice was 'I don't wanna be' by Gavin DeGraw, great tune. As soon as play resumed, I resumed a hard focus, often slightly ahead of play to ensure I was aware of any possibilities that could arise.

The one positive about this game was that we kept it goalless. On a personal level I was keeping my focus and my performance level was high, reading the game well on two occasions in the first half, making a vital save with my foot in the second half, followed by a commanding take from a far post cross towards the end of the match. Orient did miss a golden chance late on; I thought I was beaten but the ball ended up on the wrong side of the post. Full time, penalties, and time to shine.

I slowly walked to the home end, which incidentally was closed for this game. No one to try and antagonise me, well, except the two ball boys? They didn't look the gobby type though. I complimented the Orient keeper Lee Butcher on the walk, it was his full debut and he had performed very well, the lad's got a future. I even commented that this could end up being the dream debut, although despite saying it I didn't believe it. Brentford will progress in this competition, we have to for if we don't I may not feature all that much this season!

Once again our penalties were superb and so were Orient's. 5-4 up, Mathew Spring (Orient player) to take. I know 'Springy' from my Watford days, a technically gifted player. Will he smash it? Unlikely, if I know him as well as I think I do he'll look to whip it across his body similar to his free kick technique. I retreat to my line, get low, clap my hands and explode to my right. I've guessed right and see the ball heading towards my chest for me to parry away to safety, comfortable save, get in! I get up and celebrate to the empty stand, then turn and am greeted by the lads. Not quite the buzz of Everton but point made again, I'm a step closer in my pursuit.

Like a book...

Progress confirmed.

Chapter 5 - October

In truth it was the cup competitions that were keeping me going. With each victory came the promise of another game. Since Ben was cup tied I couldn't be denied the cup games. Well, that being said, technically he could play the JPT games but after playing a vital role in the first two JPT games and with it giving me the opportunity to perform - I couldn't imagine the gaffer would want the aggravation that dropping me for these games would lead to.

Looking back over the past few games I had begun to feel a shift in my thinking. I was certainly more confident and I had a surge of motivation, it was a far cry from the mind-set I often experienced in my younger days. As a younger goalkeeper I despised 'game day', to the point of wanting to quit football altogether. I actually did try to quit once only to be told that I wasn't allowed (by my dad)! Okay that's not entirely true (he didn't *forbid* me from quitting) and I'm so thankful now that he talked me around. But, honestly, I didn't know how to deal with the emotions I experienced every single time I was due to play a match.

It made no sense on so many levels. I was a talented keeper, I was highly thought of by all my coaches and held in high regard by team mates but I just couldn't understand why I would feel so jittery on a game day. My thought process prior to the game would be something along the lines of this:

"I hope I can get through today without making a mistake, although it's pretty windy which will make crosses tough to come for, and it's been raining too so the ground may be heavy which will in turn make it tough to strike from, not to mention the ball being slippery."

I would hold on to negative comments from the past (which the brain has a tendency to do, we will remember one negative comment over the many nice comments we receive). I may even begin to drift and think of a holiday I was on, and how nice the weather was, and now it's a cold, wet and windy day and I have to go and play football in it. Not only that, I'll have managers there making judgements on my every move. What if I were to say I was injured then I could avoid all this?

Then my mind would turn, and I would realise how lucky I was. There are people in the world dying of starvation, getting abused, and all the other horrible things that go on and there's me worried about a game of football. How pathetic am I?!!

This self-loathing didn't exactly inspire me or help with the anxiety!

Okay maybe I did think about a lot of things, but you can get some idea of the mental turmoil I would endure on a weekly basis! I was aware this was complete lunacy on a conscious level, and came about simply because I didn't understand my psyche. I went for a number of years experiencing high levels of anxiety and as much as I tried to pretend that I didn't care or tried to ignore it - I couldn't.

I could have quit at the age of 14, I was very close and I often ask myself the question, would it have made me happy? Well it would have made me comfortable which in turn would have led to frustration, which I would have found more distressing than my current anxiety levels.

I had obviously done something right to have got to where I was, my negative ways had served a purpose. Despite my concoction of emotions I usually played to a high standard. I put on an impressive front - no one would have known the torment going on in my head. My mind-set, although uncomfortable, had served me well to a point.

I would look at those in the dressing room with envy and again the thoughts would be present: why is it only me who experiences this? Maybe I'm not cut out for this?

In psychology there is a model called the *competence model*, the four stages being:

1. unconscious incompetence

2. conscious incompetence

3. conscious competence

4. and finally unconscious competence (being considered the pinnacle)

To be unconsciously competent at anything means that you are accomplished in that chosen pursuit and it requires little conscious awareness of what you are performing; the idea that you become so adept at something it just flows without thought. In my early years, I would fit into the first category, 'I didn't know that I didn't know', I didn't know that I could alter these feelings I experienced. I didn't know that what I was thinking was simply a manifestation of what I believed to be true. I had the power to alter my beliefs and have flexibility in my thinking but I had no awareness of this.

In a nutshell, anxiety is fear. The brain is aware that you are soon to face a situation that will take you outside of what you consider comfortable. It will then instigate the fight or flight mechanism. Some people naturally have the mentality of 'bring it on' and some say 'no thanks'. I was saying 'no thanks' and still playing! Perhaps I was too cowardly to admit to my feelings and actually go through with the decision that I wanted to make at that time? Can you imagine if I had made that decision, surely I would soon have faced another similar challenge even if it were in a different arena? Would I have run again? Would you be reading my book now?! I highly doubt it.

Something that I couldn't get my head around is that I would give everything to this game (and I kept telling myself - it is only a GAME!). We may lose, I may make a mistake and I could feel the disappointment of those around me. I may even get shouted at by a manager for making a mistake (the shouting was a regular occurrence). I have no doubt the manager would say that he's trying to 'toughen me up' but to be honest he was making me want to quit. I give him everything, we win and I'm loved. We lose and I'm despised. What a fickle world.

'Toxic thoughts' – the creation of internal chemicals

Did you know that every time you have a thought, your brain releases a chemical? I only became aware of this quite recently and it opened up a new reality to me.

This is how it works; you have a thought, your brain releases chemicals, electrical transmissions go through your brain, and you become aware of what you are thinking. If you can picture in your mind's eye the weight and power of thoughts, you will agree that they are real and they have a real impact on how you feel and how you behave. Every time you have an angry, unkind or sad thought, your brain releases negative chemicals that activate your deep limbic system and make your body feel bad. Think about the last time you were mad. How did you feel? When most people are angry their muscles become tense, hearts beat faster, their hands start to sweat, and they may even begin to feel a little dizzy.

Alternatively every time you have a good thought, a happy thought, a hopeful thought, or a kind thought, your brain releases chemicals that calm your deep limbic system and help your body feel good. Think about the last time that you were happy. How did you feel? When most people are happy their muscles relax, their hearts beat slower, their hands become dry, and they breathe more slowly. Your body also reacts to your good thoughts.

It was a destructive thought pattern that was producing my negative states and increasing anxiety. With my newfound awareness I could alter this and ensure I felt good prior to game days; I am in control of my own thoughts, so why choose to think negatively, this surely can't empower me? And like many other things in life, emotions are habitual, this being due to the fact that we will have 90%+ of the same thoughts tomorrow that we had today. This awareness allowed me to break the pattern I had formed.

Anyway more on thought patterns later, for now things were beginning to get back on track and another challenge was just around the corner in the shape of Birmingham City at St Andrews for what promised to be a memorable night.

6
November
Fourth Time Lucky

Two more games were now guaranteed: Birmingham in the Carling Cup and Swindon in the JPT. Ben would once again start the league game and fair dues to him - he was standing up to my challenge - he would keep his place against Brighton although it would end in another defeat. Rock bottom and pressure increasing on the manager by the game.

We travelled up in the morning for the Birmingham game. Game days have always intrigued me, from the second I wake up in the morning I'm aware I have a game, a feeling that I wake up with, anxiety, nerves, butterflies - whatever you want to label it as. I know I have a game. I now label it differently, it's fear.

Fear comes in all sorts of forms, the definition of fear (according to Google) is 'an unpleasant emotion caused by the belief that someone or something is dangerous, likely to cause pain, or a threat'. The promise of Birmingham City and playing in front of

Chapter 6 - November

20,000 people could be perceived as a threat to my ego if I were to play poorly.

In order to perform at a high level it's important to learn strategies to not only deal with fear but to utilise it in a constructive way. A by-product of fear is the release of adrenaline, it is adrenaline that allows you an extra few percent in performance if used wisely. It can also destroy your game if not understood. It wasn't until relatively recently that I gained a grasp of how to control my personal state, to ensure that I'm not consumed by emotions. I now give myself a few simple reminders for each game.

Game time will come when it's ready, control what is within your power, eat well, sleep well and think positive thoughts, then give everything you have come game time. That is all you can do.

"Concentrate on the present and the past will take care of itself."

Power of the present

Why worry about things that haven't happened yet? This doesn't just apply to football. The truth is that if 'things' do happen - you will deal with them. You always do and therefore worrying about something unproductive is simply time wasted. Imagery is entirely different in that the thoughts are positive, it's the idea that you actively imagine performing a task to your optimum, in the same way that you are thinking about a solution, and this is entirely different to thinking about a problem or mistake. I've done this before many a time, and this is a sure fire way to heighten fearful feelings.

Back in Birmingham, we stayed in a hotel for the afternoon, allowing time for a sleep; this is normal preparation for a night game. We arrived at St Andrews, quite dated now but still a great arena, perfect night for it too, calm, dry and a slick pitch, ideal for a good game of football.

The Brentford fans had turned up in their masses. I was unaware that this was the furthest Brentford had come in this competition for quite some time so this occasion took on further significance and they were in for some night.

Maik Taylor was Birmingham's starting goalkeeper for the night with Ben Foster given a rest on the bench. I had grown close to Ben during our time at Watford so was slightly disappointed I wouldn't get to face him but I decided to use it as an added motivation that he was there watching. My preparation had been good, I was ready, game time.

When reminiscing about the Birmingham experience I will go back to pre-game when we were walking around St Andrews, looking at the pitch and getting a feel for our surroundings. It really was a great night for football, relatively cool but so still and calm. The stadium was empty but we knew that within a matter of a couple of hours it would be rocking. I had several friends and family coming to this one and I was excited for them to see me play. I hadn't played many big games over the past few years but this would be a big one. Again I made a pact with myself, give everything, enjoy the experience and don't leave anything out there.

Work time

The first half was bright, we defended well, I was forced into a brave save early on taking the ball square in the face with it rebounding to safety. I literally didn't feel it, this being another benefit of the adrenaline present in my body. Half time was 0-0, so far so good.

Roycie gave me his customary nod of the head as I walked in for half time. I felt great again, I was striking the ball better than ever, my left foot was a wand; drilled, clipped or curled I was hitting my target and with each contribution I was aware that the bond was growing between myself and the Brentford faithful.

Enjoyment.

Second half and we were giving as good as we got. This was different to the Everton game, I wasn't under the cosh anywhere near as much, and in fact taking the first half save away this could be labelled as a quiet game. Twenty minutes to go and suddenly a shock looked on the cards, the ball drops to Sam Wood on the volley, Sam has fantastic technique and he showed it with a thumping volley into the corner. Great finish - one nil!

The site of the Brentford fans erupting as the ball hit the net will live long in the memory, the whole team celebrating in front of what must have been 3,000+ fans who had made the journey, in utter delirium. I could feel the roar resonate around what was a now shocked St Andrews.

Twenty minutes to go I repeated to myself, keep your focus. The potential of a quarter final awaits but focusing on that won't help me now, live in the present, give everything. Ten minutes remaining and I'm forced into a full stretch save to my left. Here we go, they won't give up without a fight. Birmingham's players are piling forward but we are dealing with it, minutes go by at a slow rate but we're nearly there.

The final minute arrives. We're now camped in our own half very aware of the situation we are in. A long ball gets pumped forward into our box and we fail to deal with it. It falls to Kevin Philips, the last person we would want it to fall to. I can't quite cover the distance and he tucks it away with authority, we look for an offside flag in vain, it's not coming. 1-1, instant heartbreak, and now extra time.

We had deserved to win but that's irrelevant now, it's never productive to get stuck 'in' a problem, must fight through it, keep focus - discuss after. We regroup and enter extra time with renewed vigour, this is our only option right now. It would be a travesty to crumble now.

I make a save from Zigic in the first period from point blank range, first half negotiated securely, and then the second half goes without any significant incidents. It's penalties, of course.

St Andrews, another Premier League team, the stage was set, time to be the hero. I look over to Ben Foster who was smiling; he'd seen me perform my penalty magic at Watford during his time there, building something of a reputation for it. Maik Taylor was keeping goal for the blues, a keeper I have a lot of time for, no fuss, goes about his game in a non-assuming fashion but highly effective.

This unfortunately wouldn't be another fairy tale ending. I guessed right on 4 of the 5 shots but the penalties were of a high standard. Lee Bowyer missed the 4th penalty but Taylor would save the decisive penalty from Craig Woodman. Credit to Maik in that he stood still - it's so rare to see a keeper stand still on a penalty, it was only later that I found out he had seen footage of our penalties against Everton. He'd done his homework, even more credit, top pro.

Chapter 6 - November

I felt slightly numb after the game and this feeling hung around for a couple of days. I'd played another very good game but couldn't help but think an opportunity had been missed. As a rarity I would check the paper again. As with the Everton game the Sun had awarded me a 7/10. I honestly don't think I've got an 8 in me if that's the standard!

Had I won a place in the team yet? No, I knew I was getting close though and my opportunity wouldn't be far away and in keeping with the season so far it would be dramatic!

Hunty came on during the second half of the Birmingham game but this was one of the very few appearances he had made during the season. He was also struggling to find a way into the team. Despite putting in a couple of impressive pre-season displays, including a majestic free kick against Wycombe Wanderers, he simply wasn't in favour and in truth the style of football we played wouldn't have done his game justice. He played the odd 15 minutes here and there but this wasn't enough for him, he was too good to do this and he's not the type to sit around and accept matters, he loves playing football too much. He had a discussion with the manager and they agreed he could go out on loan, which he soon did to Crawley Town, who although in the conference were as good as nailed on for promotion and had plans far bigger than that too.

A few months later David would play a starring role in their heroic attempt to defeat Manchester United at Old Trafford, losing narrowly 1-0. The next day David's picture was splashed over every paper. He was sporting Wayne Rooney's shirt as they had swapped after the game. Crawley would go on to get promotion and the loan would soon become permanent. I was saddened by his departure although I fully appreciated it was the right move for him. We were and still are close friends and even if it was only for a matter of a few months - it was great to be a teammate of his.

When you least expect it

I would normally prepare to sit on the bench in the same way I would prepare if I was playing - but today would be different. It was a Tuesday at the beginning of November and we were due to play Bournemouth. I had several deadlines that day relating to an apartment I was due to move into. I was all over the place. Eating on the go and no chance of a nap. In turn, I'm aware that it's supposedly around 50/1 that a keeper is needed when sitting on the bench. Today I've hedged my bets. I feel okay, tired but okay. If someone is up there then today they would teach me a lesson. Never assume anything!

I normally arrive very early, usually an hour or so, before I need to be at the stadium. It can be a tricky journey to Griffin Park and I certainly don't need the worry of whether I'll make it or not (not to mention the hefty fine that accompanies it). Ben Hamer had also given himself time, just not enough to account for a mass pile up on the M4.

It struck me as odd that a team talk was called 10 minutes earlier than normal, with Ben not present. The manager went through the usual tactical talk before naming the team at the very end which would leave little time for discussion as he made his way back to his office. Tactics sorted, now for the team: "In goal Richard, left back..." All I needed to hear was that first line, this was it, a league game, my first league game since November 2008. It had been two years without playing a league game of football. I thought he may call me into his office to confirm matters, I thought wrong.

'The invisible roadblock' - limiting beliefs

I like the idea that you 'create your own luck'. It is purely a belief but this belief opens the mind to the idea that the harder you work, the luckier you get. This however is a belief and doesn't make it right or wrong, my thinking is simply that it is more beneficial for me to believe that I am lucky than unlucky. By believing I am unlucky I will search for circumstances that back up that belief. I could become a 'victim', I will be the guy who 'would have, if only this or that had gone my way', or I can choose to believe in ideas that will help me in a constructive way. I believe I am lucky and the harder I train the more luck will be heaped upon me, this empowers me.

Hard at work...

I am acutely aware now that beliefs are a choice, you can choose what you wish to believe about anyone or anything. The basic principle for success is to arrange those beliefs in a way that will empower you and not limit you. Would it benefit me to think I am terrible goalkeeper or a fantastic keeper? Well, thinking that I am a terrible keeper it may lead to feelings of inadequacy and a lack of motivation. On the flip side that very same belief may get me thinking that I must work harder than others in order to compete, therefore in a bizarre way it is still empowering. Whilst believing I am excellent may lead to increased confidence, it could also lead to an unfounded arrogance and a detrimental effect on performance. Beliefs have the power to help you excel or destroy you, and we are all different in how we arrange our beliefs to help us excel.

A huge part of not only football but life is to gain awareness over your beliefs. Do they allow me to succeed or do they limit me? The same idea to you could mean something completely different to someone else, my challenge has been to find the beliefs that best suit me and which allow me to perform at my very best.

Mohammed Ali is one of the best examples of having an unwavering belief in himself. He truly believed he was destined for greatness and he wasn't shy in telling others!

"I believe I am destined for greatness."

I like this statement for several reasons. Firstly by airing it you are forming a verbal contract with whoever you decide to tell, ideally this will be someone who will remind you of this when necessary! Secondly in adopting this belief it's important you raise your standards instantly, to say it and maintain average standards could make you look foolish. Some may initially take this as an arrogant remark but providing you can back it up in a similar way to that of Mohammed Ali with hard work and dedication then you will be on the right path. It will be ingrained in you and you'll settle for nothing less. The first step to being great is believing that you can be.

Ben arrived and wasn't happy. My theory is that the manager knew I deserved a start and was looking for an excuse to start me. Players were late all the time, why punish Ben now? This did however give him the excuse he needed.

I wasn't feeling at my best but this presented a nice challenge in much of what I'd learned. Despite having had a busy day and not preparing to my optimum could I still play to my potential? I had reframed instantly; I viewed this as an exciting challenge and allowed myself no excuses.

The game itself went okay. In truth it was a quiet game, we went one down but soon equalised. I kicked solidly, read the game well and took some tough high balls, one each the final score. I was pleased. In years gone by I may have pointed to the fact that I wasn't at my peak but without realising it I was sabotaging myself. Who cares what my reasons are, we could all find a million reasons as to why we didn't do something well. The fact of the matter is that I didn't do it well: don't get stuck in a problem, find a way to deal with that problem and come out the other side.

We were now faced with two cup games. This meant that I would be sure to start both matches but in my mind it meant I had two games to ensure that I started against MK Dons in our next league fixture.

First up - Aldershot in the FA Cup. The tables had now turned in that this was a game we were *expected* to win unlike the mammoth displays against Everton and Birmingham. We were poor and could only draw the game; I was awarded the man of the match accolade although I think this was more an insult to us as a team than an acknowledgement of any personal performance. I was solid and growing in consistency but I barely had a save to make. Nevertheless I happily accepted the prize and the free meal for two awarded with it.

You can't get me up here.

Soon after the Aldershot match, Swindon awaited in the JPT. I was as good as guaranteed this game. The game wasn't great, we went one down early on but equalised towards the end of the half. Swindon dominated the second half, I made several saves to once again take it to penalties, the fourth time this season! I had lost the previous one to Birmingham and wouldn't allow for it to be two in a row.

As it turned out I wasn't needed, they missed the target on two of their four spot kicks so we progressed comfortably. It felt slightly odd when the lads rushed over to celebrate with me bearing in mind that I hadn't actually saved a penalty! I guess it was habit now. When winning a shootout the keeper gets mobbed regardless, it's always nice nonetheless!

It was clear that the manager was under severe pressure, this victory was visibly important to him; ironically it was the cup competitions that were keeping him in his job right now.

**Audition for the annual
Brentford FC three-legged race...**

I would keep my place in the team for the next fixture, and this
was a boost. As far as I was concerned the place was now mine
to lose and having fought so hard to get it I certainly wasn't
intending on giving it up easily. The next game would result in a
2-0 defeat to MK Dons, but again I played well and picked up
another Man of the Match award.

Meal for 6 now, any takers?

Purple patch

A good run soon followed. We beat Plymouth on the road (never an easy place to go to) and followed that up with a 2-0 victory over Colchester at Layer road. We were creeping up the table. As each game came and went I soon found myself forming an understanding with those in front of me, something very important to any successful defensive unit.

Over the course of the season I certainly found myself bonding with my two centre halves. Leon Legge is a monster of a man, any long ball played in his vicinity he will head and more often than not he'll head the ball further than it's just been kicked! Karleigh Osborne has all the attributes needed to make it to the top: a wand of a right foot, speed, and strength in abundance. On the flanks, Craig Woodman at left back was as consistent a performer as we had throughout the whole season. More often than not it would be Kev O'Connor occupying the right back spot, the veteran utilising his endless years of experience and deploying his know how to ensure we were a conducive unit. (Years of experience? It really is the only banter I have for him.)

We began to form an understanding, clearing up a lot of danger before it developed and eventually being able to boast a record of conceding less than 1 goal per game in the games we played. Only Southampton would end up having a better record in League One.

Speaking of Southampton, they were next on our fixture list. Away, at St Mary's. It doesn't get much tougher.

7

December Goalkeeper of the Month

Southampton away posed a huge challenge, a team who looked set for a return to the Championship and in truth a team who were very much prepared to do so.

I've played at Southampton a couple of times previously and love playing there, the surface is always great, so easy to strike a ball off due to the nature of the turf and the stadium is set for a return to the Premier League let alone the Championship. I had actually played there for Watford two years before and made two penalty saves in one game. We won that game 3-0, although I had no doubt today would be a tougher challenge.

Five minutes in and I produce my save of the season, a bullet header from 6 yards - I flung both hands up instinctively to parry the ball onto the bar and over. No idea how I'd got to it but delighted that I had. Perhaps it was destined to be a good day.

An uncharacteristic mistake by the usually reliable Kelvin Davis gave us an unlikely lead which we soon doubled. On the stroke of half time I plunged to my left to get fingertips to a ball bound for the bottom left hand corner, the deflection would see it brush the post on the way for a corner. The travelling Brentford faithful were there in their masses and they were enjoying this one. I made several more saves in what would turn out to be a fantastic 2-0 victory; it also set a new Brentford record of five away wins in a row.

Bob Patmore, a mentor I will speak of in more detail shortly was present at this game and he would give me a lift home after the match. When meeting with Bob the subject would regularly go to that of the mind and processes by which we can utilise the mind to produce the results we desire. He would often speak of an outcome based mindset, something that struck a chord with me and something which made a whole lot of sense. Bob had several great examples, and I recently had one of my own.

Outcome based mindset

The lesson I learnt was thanks to a visit to a well loved local Indian restaurant. The food there is great but the service is dreadful, and every time I go there it seems to get worse to the point where I actually walked out recently. After sitting and waiting for service of any kind (for what seemed an eternity) and not even being asked what we were drinking, 'we' being my girlfriend Holly and I. The decision was made that they didn't deserve our business so we walked out. We made our point, and I'm sure when we tell everyone of our actions they'll all give us a hearty 'good on you' for doing what was right in that circumstance, fantastic.

The problem was that I was really looking forward to eating Indian food. At that time nothing else was on my mind and there wasn't another Indian restaurant in close proximity. My desired outcome was simply that I would be eating Indian food for lunch and, although I felt some sense of self-worth for 'showing them', I had failed in my outcome. I had spited myself in order to make a point. In hindsight I would have been far more satisfied had I have eaten the meal and perhaps made a mental note of the experience for future reference or better still provided feedback for the restaurant staff.

My realisation was this: sometimes things may not go as I intend them to go. Flexibility in any approach is important and providing I have clarity over what it is that I want at the end of the process, and I find a way to get it - then success has been achieved.

Soon after Southampton we faced Charlton in what was effectively the quarter final of the JPT and what would rank up there with the Everton experience. Initially it wasn't certain I would play this game, Ben Hamer was unhappy with the way he had been treated and wanted another shot. He spoke with the manager a couple of weeks prior to the Charlton game and was promised he would be given this game. This kept Ben quiet for a couple of weeks, but as the big day approached – he found out he wouldn't play the Charlton game. Frankly, *I* would have been livid had *I* not been given the Charlton game; I had been instrumental in our cup run and now with this game live on Sky I felt I had a right to play. The gaffer had caused himself more issues.

As footballers, or anyone for that matter, all you ask is that you are given honest feedback by a manager or boss. You won't please everyone, but we are all men, we'll deal with it, we have to. Whatever the reason it certainly wasn't just me who felt the right amount of feedback was lacking, and it was causing problems in the dressing room. The only saving grace was that we were (thankfully) getting positive results.

Preparation was now following a similar pattern for each game. The night before would mean a high carb dinner followed by a concoction of pills required to mask the pain in my knee. To be precise it's a mixture of Diclofenac (an anti-inflammatory) and glucosamine that I take. I take a maximum dosage of Diclofenac (150mg) following the operation to remove the meniscus in my knee, and find that the amount of exercise I do must be monitored in order to control the persistent swelling I get. I have grown concerned of late as to what the pills are doing to my insides - regular bouts of diarrhoea and fatigue suggest that they're doing me no favours. They are however very effective. Following food and medication, I get a good night's sleep. Afterwards, the process of channelling my thoughts where possible prior to each game ensures I am as ready I can possibly be.

Penalty perfection

The Charlton game was poor. Sky TV was present and I'm sure they would have regretted choosing this match as the one they would air. For the fifth time this season (for Brentford) it would go to penalties.

Roycie had done his homework and told me that their first taker, Johnny Jackson would go straight down the middle. I very rarely stand still for a penalty and I wouldn't have done this ordinarily but I trusted Roycie on this one. He was spot on, Jackson hit it true but I reacted in time to get both hands to it, one save made.

It begins.

I had no other information on the Charlton players but I felt so powerful. I was utilising everything I had learned, my body language was now spot on, chest out, hard focus and turning all that adrenaline coursing through me into explosive power.

Therry Racon stepped up, I had a hunch he would come across me but it was nothing more than a hunch. I clapped my hands loudly on the run up, I was crouched low, like a coiled spring. He struck it well but I had read him and exploded to my right powerfully. I extended my arm to flick it up onto the post and away. Two saves.

Chapter 7 - December

**I saved the ball but failed in blocking
out the blinding floodlight...**

I was 'on it' or as psychologists would call it, I was well and truly 'in the zone'. The state in which you barely think, you don't need to, it all comes so naturally. You are at one with what is going on.

Kyel Reid approached. I was dripping with arrogance - Lionel Messi could step up now and I'd save his penalty. I strutted over, never have I felt so energetic with such a pure focus. I looked into his eyes hoping that in some way I would be given a psychic signal as to where he would go. It may not have been psychic powers that made me decide to go right but that was where I was going to dive, mind made up, now commit to the dive.

He fired high to my right, much higher than the previous penalty, I had dived mid height but managed to readjust to get my left palm to the ball, it was a strong hand but I was aware I hadn't fully blocked it, it was spinning back towards the goal, I got up and sprinted across. I wasn't going to make it, it was rolling so slowly but I was helpless, the crowd had initially cheered the save but everyone fell silent for a split second as the ball crept towards the line at a painfully slow pace. I was running as fast as I could but I was never much of a sprinter. I always felt as though I was running at an immense speed only to see video footage of myself and realise that it was equivalent to a steady jog for most. The ball would beat me to the goal, it looked as though it may nestle in the corner, then there he was - my saviour on so many occasions - the goalpost. Never have I loved a cylindrical metal object so passionately.

Three in a row.

I thumped the ball in delight and would pick up another man of the match award presented by Sky Sports. I would also feature on Soccer AM the following week for 'incredible tekkers'. The season had certainly turned in my favour. Ben would soon return to Reading after this game.

This time I felt more worthy of the 'mobbing'.

Table for 8 please…

Penalty prowess

It is perhaps no surprise that I have a habit for saving penalties over the years when I tell you of one of my earliest memories as a goalkeeper. It was my first season between the sticks at the age of 9 and we faced league leaders Belgrave. I was playing for my local team at the time – Bedgrove Dynamos - and this game has forever stuck in the memory. This was the first game that I felt like the hero. One nil down at the time and we faced a penalty. I remember diving low to my left to make the save and for us to fight back and win the game 2-1. I was given 'man of the match' and remember the feeling – the feeling of real significance. To me at that time playing football well equalled attention, and that was fine by me.

I can't quite understand why my Mum would dress me like a 65 year old.

Such a full head of hair (sigh...).

Despite only playing two games in December, I got nominated for the League One player of the month award, the only goalkeeper nominated, and another welcome massage for the ego. I knew I was in a good state right now, feeling fit and motivation levels were high.

Reinforcement

I had just been to the cinema to watch a film that had intrigued me for many reasons, the film was called *The Social Network*. In particular, one scene that stuck in my mind was a discussion between would-be-multi-billionaire founder Mark Zuckerberg and Sean Parker. Sean Parker gave his motivation for his creation of Napster, a world renowned website for downloading free music. The story, as it goes, is that he was besotted with a girl who was with one of the 'jocks' in his class. His thinking was simple. Create something extraordinary and in doing so 'win the girl'. He did the first part and in doing so the second part became an irrelevance. The motivation was simply the vehicle needed to help him get to where he intended going. I could see similarities in my initial desire to become a footballer – the girl named Charlotte who was my primary motivation factor as a young goalkeeper; my thought process being that footballers 'get the girl'. I never did, in the case of Charlotte, and inevitably this was an irrelevance, however it strengthened my belief that there is no right or wrong motivation, a big enough 'reason why' and I know I'll find a way.

The heavy snow that Britain experienced in December caused havoc for the following three weeks or so. Game after game was called off and very little training could be done. It was clear that we would have a fixture pile up in 2011. We were on a good run that had helped propel us up the table and to within touching distance of the playoffs. It was well known that our manager was applying for other jobs and, as rumour would have it, he was near certain for a move to become Sheffield United's manager. In the end, however, Sheffield opted for Mickey Adams instead.

Despite our form it was still an unhappy camp, the turnaround of players was somewhat embarrassing. I felt like I was one of the longer serving players - having lasted 6 months.

Life altering memories

During this period I had the opportunity to return to Vicarage Road and watch Watford, the under-soil heating ensuring that their game against Leicester City would beat the weather. As a guest for the day and being initiated into the 'Legends Lounge' (a title that I certainly wouldn't bestow upon myself but I appreciated the sentiment) I would also get to join Richard Short on the pitch at half time for a chat. I was delighted to receive a nice ovation on the first time I had returned to the 'Vic' since leaving.

Meeting Elton John, a privilege.

I walked off the pitch, signed a few autographs, spoke to a few regulars I had gotten to know over my years at the club, and in the process was reminded of many memories I had experienced with the club. The key ones being the double penalty save I had made against Southampton and my performance away to Manchester City. However, I was thankful that no one mentioned our failed play off attempt in 2008.

The play off attempt I speak of was a significant turning point during my time at Watford, one that would take me a while to recover from, yet one that I would now consider one of the best lessons I could have received.

I had played the majority of the 2007/8 season which would lead to us making the play offs. On the face of things I had enjoyed a very positive season, ousting Mart Poom for the number one spot, captaining the team for 8 unbeaten games, playing 38 games in total as well as coming third for player of the season. Yet, despite all this, one moment would leave me mentally scarred for some time.

We played Hull away in the second leg of our play off tie. We were two down from the first leg but got ourselves a goal to give us a chance and we were very much in the ascendancy. I remember a long ball played through which was headed high in the air, my first instinct was that I could claim this ball but as it began to drop I realised I wasn't getting there. I was in 'no-man's land'. I tried to recover but it was to no avail as the ball was headed over me and nestled in the back of the net. We would lose the game 4-1. Despite not being at fault for any further goals I had crumbled. The stadium was full, it was live on Sky and I felt entirely to blame. Their fourth goal was greeted with a pitch invasion; I wanted the ground to swallow me up. The 37 good games beforehand paled into insignificance. I felt dreadful.

This feeling of guilt would stay with me well into the following season and I was duly demoted to third choice keeper before an unexpected chance would present itself. Two keepers injured in the same week, surely that's unheard of? I wasn't ready to play and the inconsistency of my game showed that. One week I saved three penalties and played two of my best ever games followed by a run of four of the worst games I'd ever played. I didn't want to be there, I didn't want to play football anymore. I had hit a new low. I hated football more than ever. This was the moment I knew I needed to change my approach or find a new job. I set upon a process of changing my approach.

Someone who was instrumental in helping me do this was the next of my four mentors, Keith Mincher.

Chapter 7 - December

Keith Mincher

On a monthly basis I will call on Keith Mincher. I met Keith under Aidy Boothroyd's tenure at Watford FC; he was psychologist / performance coach who rightly was heavily praised following Watford's rise to the Premier League in 2006. Although I had read a few books on the mind, Keith would play a huge role in showing me the path to self-fulfilment and contentment. On the back of his recommendation I attended two Anthony Robbins seminars, a guy who is largely considered to be one of the world's premier performance coaches. I was fascinated with book after book that Keith recommended and most recently I became a practitioner of NLP (Neuro Linguistic Programming) myself. He certainly helped open my mind to other possibilities and more than that helped me gain a greater awareness of myself and my mental setup.

Talking to Keith would be a different conversation to other mentors I engage with. Keith is a master practitioner in NLP and has incredible knowledge of the mind. With each conversation I always ensure I have a pad and pen at hand in order to feed off the wisdom of such an educated man.

Quality of your question

'The quality of your questions determine the quality of your life'. This nugget of wisdom was first shared with me by Keith, and in truth I didn't understand it at first. The questions he refers to don't always have to be *to* someone else, more often than not it will be *your* thoughts. Self talk can be hugely destructive if the questions you ask yourself are geared in such a way that there is no positive outcome. I became aware of some of my own self talk, for example, I would previously ask myself 'why am I not in the team?' which would in turn lead to me reeling off a list of things that I wasn't particularly good at, and not feeling overly great about myself.

Alternatively the question 'what can I do in order to get into the team and ensure I stay there?' is the same question but constructed in a way that offers hope and inspiration. Ask a bad question and more often than not you will receive a bad answer.

I remember being told once that you become like those who you associate with; the idea being that when in a group of people, often friends, you will unconsciously hold each other back from progressing too far. This dynamic changes when those who you associate with are performing at a higher level than you. Keith is performing at the highest level, and that being the case I consider myself incredibly fortunate to be able to associate myself with him and in turn aid my personal growth.

The excessive snow meant a Christmas off for the first time in years. The usual preparations for Boxing Day were not required so I returned back home to stay with Mum, Dad and my three brothers. 2011 was now around the corner and plenty more twists and turns awaited.

8

January
A Month is a Long Time
in Football

We would beat Dagenham on New Year's Day but this would be our last victory for a while. Defeats to Bournemouth, Yeovil and Peterborough would put a halt to our good run.

Next up was the semi final of the JPT or the 'Area Final' as it was called and the chance to play at Wembley for the victors. Exeter stood in our way. The Area Final was a two legged affair. We were on a terrible run and needed to turn our fortunes around sharpish otherwise we could lose this tie in the first leg.

My previous few games had been average at best. I made what I considered to be my first mistake of the season (misreading a cross) against Yeovil and had struggled with my kicking against Peterborough.

Chapter 8 - January

After the Peterborough game I was interviewed and asked whether I thought that if Ben Hamer still been at the club he would have won his place back (on the back of my previous two performances). I wasn't impressed with the question in the slightest; I wanted to rip into the interviewer and remind him of the countless man of the match performances I had secured, and ask whether a couple of bad kicks and misreading a cross at Yeovil warranted being dropped? However I said something along the lines of: "Obviously we're all disappointed with our performance over the past two games and we'll do all we can to put it right". Being aggressive wouldn't have done me any favours.

Now, I don't like to be criticised, no one does. A technique I've formed over the years is to detach myself from my game - the thought being that I am more than my profession and I won't let it define me. Admittedly this can be tough, when meeting someone, one of the first things I will be asked is 'what I do'. Of course this is natural, I'm proud of my career and I will tell people that I play football, but making a mistake doesn't make me a bad person. Likewise a great performance doesn't elevate me above others. My belief is simple, I love who I am, I love the variety of my pursuits and I'm content in the life I lead. People can and will criticise my game, everyone is welcome to an opinion, the difference now being that I won't take this personally.

Motivation can come in many forms, not all of which would be considered 'pure'. Often an 'I'll show you' motivation can be just as powerful as simply having a love for your pursuit. I certainly had some of this going on after being dropped. I would wake up each day with a surge rushing through me, intent on proving how good I was and proving to the manager he was wrong in his actions. However the strangest thing happened when I finally did win a place in the team. Initially the same motivation was still present as I was by no means a sure-fire starter but as games progressed and I cemented my place in the team I could sense that the manager was pleased with me. Although he never apologised for his initial actions I was aware things had changed. Suddenly I didn't have to prove that he was wrong. Now I had to prove he was right.

This may seem odd but I was uncomfortable with this. I had become accustomed to feeling the fire in my stomach, intent on showing the world what I was about. I had now done that to a point. So what now? I needed a new 'why'!

Fighting chance

The past is the past. I can't affect it but I could affect how I approached the semi final, and I did want to play at Wembley. Wembley was very much on my 'to do' list - as big a motivation as I could possibly ask for.

Exeter would prove to be a tough test, a team renowned for playing good football and a team on a considerably better run than we were. The Sky cameras were once again present, which always adds a sense of tension around the place. Players are aware when the Sky cameras are present, some players like the added edge, some do not. Some see it as an opportunity, others as an unwanted pressure. Despite a couple of disappointing games I was in a place where I wanted the cameras there, I wanted to show what I could do.

The weather did not provide ideal goalkeeping conditions: heavy wind and rain, not to mention a low temperature which could play havoc on what was now a heavily cut up Griffin Park pitch. These however would be excuses, it is the same for both teams, I can't control the elements. I can control my mind-set, remain positive, give everything and enjoy it regardless. Contract with myself agreed, let's play ball.

I made several saves in the first half, one a full stretch fingertip save to my left I was particularly proud of, and managed to help keep the score down to one. The atmosphere in the dressing room at half time wasn't healthy. The manager was once again in the firing line and his persona magnified that. There was nothing calm and calculated about his approach, more screaming and shouting, he was frustrated and his words weren't affecting us in a positive way. We had to somehow galvanise ourselves otherwise this tie would be over before the long away trip to Exeter.

We needed a miracle of sorts. We were in danger of losing heavily. I made several more saves before we were given a slice of fortune. A punch by Paul Jones would land at the feet of Myles who crossed the ball to Gaz Alexander to slot home. An ugly game but we had salvaged a draw. Not an ideal result at home but something to give us a fighting chance at Exeter in a fortnight's time.

Before the second game was to be played - Exeter made a surprise signing: Ben Hamer from Reading! Ben who had been so badly treated by Andy Scott was now due to play against us, and having not played in the Charlton game he was eligible to play for Exeter in the second leg. After the way Ben had been treated surely defeating us would be some form of karmic justice? This wasn't the mindset to have however; my mindset was simply that I deserved this, a day at Wembley, years of dedication to a noble pursuit and the promise of playing on the hallowed turf only a game away.

Prior to the second leg against Exeter, though, we had several key games that could either propel us back into playoff contention, or mean a relegation dog fight.

Yeovil at home first up. I'd spent all week feeling under the weather but was sure I'd be okay for the Saturday. I wasn't. All the positive thinking in the world couldn't help me! I just couldn't stop coughing and it wasn't pretty what I was coughing up! My body temperature was all over the place and I wasn't the only one. Gaz Alexander was also struggling, it was quite a bizarre sight - both of us sat in the changing room with silver foil wrapped around us to keep us warm. We weren't about to pull out though; this was a big game, we were perilously close to finding ourselves in a relegation dogfight. I felt horrible, I had slept about an hour in total the night before, I was cold and drained of all energy. Again, must reframe, it's a challenge, if you can play when feeling like this then you'll never have such an issue again.

A career first

The game was tough but I was just about getting through it. I decided not to shout at the same intensity as I would normally do, I just didn't have the energy. Instead, I chose my communications carefully and conserved energy where possible.

The score stood at 1-1 with 10 minutes remaining and Karleigh attempted to pass the ball back but didn't make true contact on what was now a truly awful surface. I sprinted out to try to get to the ball before the striker. I threw myself at his feet, but he made it to the ball first and in an attempt to slide the ball past me I stopped it with my arm. I tried to pretend it was my chest although I've never been a great actor, and guilt was written all over me. 'Did the ref see?' Yeah he saw, he blew his whistle, red card.

The first red card of my career and it was an odd feeling. In a twisted kind of way it was a relief to get off the field so I could get to the changing room and relax. I would go home that night and stay in bed for several days, the suspension actually doing me some good in allowing me recovery time.

We lost that game, the winner ironically coming from the free kick awarded for my hand ball. I would be suspended for the midweek encounter away to Dagenham, and this was now a 'do or die' match for Andy Scott. We all knew it. His persona was of a man who was frustrated, perhaps frustrated that he didn't get the Sheffield United job that he looked odds on to get, and also frustrated that we were on such a poor run of form. The problem was that we were still doing the same things game in game out and if nothing changes, well then how do you expect a poor run of form to change?

A quote that I am very fond of is:

"Do what you've always done and get what you've always got."

A simple quote but with so much truth attached to it. Things won't change unless you adapt your approach. If something is working well then by all means continue with what you are doing, if something isn't working then continual change is a must until you get the desired result.

"Figure out what you want, figure out why you want it, figure out how to get it, continue to adapt your approach until you get it."

As a budding goalkeeper, in my haphazard way, I was following this formula. But, something else I was doing (without realising it) was modelling excellence. I had several goalkeepers who I studied, I had utmost admiration for them and in hindsight I have no doubt they played a major part in my progression.

Model excellence

A large part of NLP is the idea of modelling excellence and for me this is essential in order to reach the top. The simple idea is this: someone has achieved something you haven't, they already know the route and can be of massive guidance to you *regardless* of whether you know them or not.

If you already know them then that is great, I would advise you to extract what information you can from them directly. They have already provided a route to get to where you want to go - be inquisitive, ask questions, listen and learn. More often than not people will be happy to help you and may even act as a mentor and help you reach your own goals.

I've been very fortunate in that the someone I modelled was very close to me. It was, in fact, my dad - Peter Lee.

My dad

Let me give you a brief background into my father. He didn't do particularly well at school but upon leaving he set upon making a success of himself in the business world. He started by opening some record stores which helped place him on the map, then he sold his company to Ritz Video and became their MD. Several years later and after opening in excess of 700 stores Ritz was bought out by Blockbuster. Dad had 'made it', he bought the house of his dreams and had enough money to live comfortably for a long while. Despite all this, however, he wasn't satisfied and needed a new goal.

He had a few not so successful ventures before joining Twins Enterprise Worldwide Ltd (now 47 Brand). When he joined he helped take the business to new heights, far surpassing what had been done before. He would then do a similar job with the headwear company New Era before again getting somewhat bored, and in need of a new challenge. He is now set to do a similar thing with his latest company Refuel who distribute brands such as Mitchell & Ness, and Starter, all over Europe (www.refuelstore.com). He also has licenses to produce headwear for many of the top football clubs (including Man City!).

My belief is that my dad naturally has many mental processes that allow him to succeed. He is very assertive in his ways and flexible in his approach. I've been fortunate to have enjoyed a great childhood and couldn't have hoped for a better role model in doing so. Strong values and highly driven, I have no doubt that many of my ways are derived from him. The only thing I didn't get from him was his 6ft 4in frame!

And I'm on tip toes...

We can also model people we don't know. I say this in that I would advise you to model the best, and the beauty of the best is that they are generally in the public domain, whether it be via Google or on TV - you'll be able to find valuable information.

My personal story on modelling excellence is actually quite unique and I'm sure you'll appreciate the thought behind it. As a young goalkeeper wanting to reach the heady heights of the Premier League I would watch Peter Schmeichel more than anyone else. This giant of a man was my hero, however it was apparent from an early age that I may not have his physical attributes, so I asked myself, what do I need to do in order to be as good as Peter Schmeichel?

Think outside the box

My view has always been that goalkeeping is visually the most impressive position on the pitch, for a large man to hang horizontally in the air whilst catching a football is some feat, and with that in mind I began to think outside the box. I could never match Peter Schmeichel physically but there are many components needed to make a top goalkeeper and one that instantly appealed to me was the idea of having fantastic spring. With increased spring I could make even more phenomenal saves, reach the very top corners, and be a huge asset to any team.

This line of thinking led me to the sport of Basketball. Why basketball? Well my theory was this, they can jump higher than most athletes (other than high jumpers of course, I just didn't think their technique was congruent to that of a goalkeeper!) so I began to watch more basketball, and look at the likes of Michael Jordan and more recently Kobe Bryant or LeBron James. *Power, speed and spring*. If, somehow, I could harness what they have and mould it into goalkeeping I could be unstoppable. I searched Google, hundreds of sites came up offering a similar idea: 'improve your spring by 'x' inches in 3 weeks'. Perfect. I remember spending £2.99 on an eBook containing a variety of basketball drills, which I still do today and my spring did improve. I was quicker, stronger and in turn far more valuable.

Linked with this training I also knew it was important to keep pushing the boundaries in order to avoid making any drill comfortable. A simple model for improvement in anything is to stretch comfort zones. If you can squat 100kg with ease then you need to move the weight up, remaining at 100kg won't generate improvement.

"The more you learn, the more you earn."

This beauty of this quote is that it can be attached to almost any pursuit and moulded accordingly. To continually 'add value' to yourself is essential to success. Adding value may be as simple as improving your diet or it may be taking an educational course that gives you an edge. Having the ability to think outside the box and hit upon ideas that could improve you - will offer you the chance of fulfilling your potential.

An idea I did take from watching Peter Schmeichel was that there were many ways to be an effective goalkeeper. Schmeichel was unorthodox in some of his ways but he was so effective, he played with personality and authority. I may not be able to match his physical presence but there were certainly elements of his game I could feed from.

Back to reality

The month drew to a close, it was tense times, we were slipping closer to the drop zone with the only glimmer of hope being the second leg of the JPT. However, we weren't playing at all well, confidence was incredibly low throughout the squad, and the brand of football we were playing didn't impress anyone.

For me, what was going on at the club signified everything that is wrong with the English game. We're proud of our British tenacity but how far can that get you in today's game? Creativity is a huge part of football, yet young players trying tricks can be berated for 'show boating' and it's gradually trained out of them. Yes the game can be physical and it is agreed that an element of steel is needed but it's also vital that a team has a 'match winner'.

I was delighted to see how well Adel Taarabt was doing at QPR - frustrating at times maybe, but give him the freedom to express himself and reap the rewards. He's an artist in his own right, one moment of magic is often enough to win a game, without that spark - teams can become one dimensional, which is often the case below the Premiership. A bunch of teams playing a similar style of football. Some will get on a good run which, if sustained, may see them make the play offs, others experience just the opposite and get pulled into the fight that inevitably ensues. We were amongst this large group, painfully average.

Something needed to change.

Blog III

Keepers Get A Raw Deal! (January 2008)

After watching Liverpool face Man Utd something became quite apparent to me: keepers really do get a raw deal! It wasn't this game alone that guided me to this conclusion but it was more apparent in this game than most.

Van der Sar didn't have his finest afternoon but the commentators were quick to pounce on his mistakes and offered little credit when it was deserved - yet later in the game Robbie Keane missed a good chance and instead of criticism, the comment made was: "Don't worry about it Robbie, they'll come soon and once they do they'll come like buses". Far kinder than the words used to describe Van der Sar's mishap which ranged from "shocking", to "catastrophic"!

It seems to me that when a striker misses a good chance it is very rare that they get pulled up on it. Maybe I am biased being a keeper myself but it disappointed me to see Reina make a fantastic tip over the bar and 90 per cent of the credit went to whoever it was taking the shot and not Reina.

The save itself was very good for a few reasons; it was a bouncing ball which meant Reina instantly read the situation and dropped three yards expecting a dipping volley - had he not made this movement then the situation would have undoubtedly ended in a goal. A small detail but a crucial one, one that many commentators wouldn't have a clue whether it had even occurred. Then the save itself needed some incredible agility and acrobatics which were almost a given. In fact, Reina was faultless all afternoon and some of his distribution was awesome and went without mention.

In my opinion the problem on this occasion was that all the pundits and commentators involved were outfield players before they retired. This is quite common and it often leads to some bizarre analysis of goalkeepers. It can be quite frustrating being a goalkeeper and knowing exactly why a keeper has done what he has done and having some ex-centre forward explaining what he believes should have been done!

I don't want to sound like a bitter keeper because I'm really not, we all understand what to expect when becoming a goalkeeper, you really do put yourself in the firing line.

I guess my only wish would be to have more goalkeeping pundits to offer a different point of view but there seem to be very few of them about currently. This will change, this must change.

9

February
A Fresh Start

I was at home watching the scores come in on the Tuesday night, still not feeling great from the weekend but a few days in bed had helped. I knew the enormity of the game against Dagenham so was keeping a close eye on the score. Goal flash, one nil Dagenham, it remained that way until half time. Could the lads dig in over the second half and salvage something? Unfortunately not, three goals in quick succession turned it into a romp. We would lose 4-1. By the Thursday morning both Andy Scott and Terry Bullivant were relieved of their duties.

I was frustrated both for, and by, Andy Scott. No one likes to see anyone lose their job and despite our run-ins I was saddened by his departure. I was frustrated by him in that this was someone who has fantastic football knowledge and on the rare occasions we did speak, I liked him. His downfall for me was that he didn't communicate well with us as a group, and his lack of flexibility in approach would ultimately let him down.

I guess the situation with me summed things up to a large extent. Within weeks of bringing me in I had been cast aside with little feedback, several of us were. I honestly think improved communication to the squad and the situation would have been different. To keep a player guessing about his status will lead to squad unhappiness. This doesn't mean daily chats to players but surely, when it's appropriate, a word is needed? Football is like any other business in so many ways; the manager heads a group of staff/players and needs to get the very best from those people.

I'd been fortunate to work with the likes of Malky Mackay and Brendan Rogers prior to my move to Brentford. To me it is no surprise that both of these men are succeeding in the way they are, and they will continue to. Intelligent men but far more than that they realise the importance of treating each player as an individual person and with empathy. I'll always remember something Brendan said to me, he said that when you talk to anyone, do so with the idea that they have 'make me feel good' tattooed to their forehead. Brendan did this, he cared for his squad, and in return his squad fought for him. I had several discussions with both of these men and Malky even dropped me during his time at Watford but I could accept it. Managers have tough decisions to make, all I asked for was honest feedback.

Much of this comes down to rules we consciously or unconsciously make and live by. When someone doesn't obey a rule we have, then we'll often experience anger or frustration. The tricky part to this is that although many of us will have similar rules, there will always be differences. I'm fully aware that part of the issue was that our rules didn't align, I doubt whether any manager would intentionally want valued players to feel unwanted.

I remember someone once telling me that most people live the way they *think* life should be led. Combined with this is the theory that most people believe what they think we should *all* believe. Now this is fine but it's apparent that we all have different models of the world and therefore won't agree on all matters and this is where this awareness is very powerful.

Rules - map of the world

One of the biggest lessons I learnt from the NLP course I attended was appreciating that we all have a different map of the world, different ideas on how to live life and the components that make up one's life. This is very apparent in football and for me it was a realisation that it's important to know how a manager operates and what he wants from a player. All managers operate differently and it's important to figure out what it is, *exactly,* that they are looking for. An example I had with Aidy Boothroyd at Watford was being aware that a goalkeeper who could distribute was very important to him. My distribution wasn't great at the time so I knew what I needed to do in order to be a goalkeeper he could work with. Appreciating his model of a goalkeeper was important to know so that I could improve my chances under his reign, and thankfully I went on to play many games under him. The principle is apparent in everyday situations, some people may deem it to be totally unacceptable if you are late for a meeting, whereas others may be completely laid back about the whole thing. There is no right or wrong but an inflexible approach can really antagonise others which in turn could jeopardise your opportunities.

Transition

Nicky Forster, our 37 year old veteran striker, would take charge until a managerial successor could be found and in doing so, he announced his retirement as a player. Mark Warburton who I had briefly got to know during his spell as Academy manager at Watford a few years back would assist Nicky.

The big surprise in regards to the sacking of Andy Scott - was the timing of it. It was before our second date with Exeter in the cup and the chance of a Wembley final. The fact of the matter was, however, that we were only two points outside the relegation zone and on current form Wembley dreams were a distant hope.

Renewed hope

Nicky and Mark took to the job at hand instantly. Their time might have been limited but that didn't stop them making some much needed improvements around the place. Training was far more structured and of a higher tempo. We would now do gym work as a standard procedure before training, as well as urine tests to ensure we were all properly hydrated for the training. A new kitchen was installed and the eating area updated. We were also informed that we would now travel to the Exeter game the day before, and stay in a hotel (as opposed to the plan of travelling on the day which would have meant a 5am wake up). Small changes maybe but all were effective and had an instant impact.

The organisation we were in had now changed, standards had risen. Am I saying that the installation of a new kitchen would help us play better? Maybe, maybe not. What it does say, however, is that we are a professional establishment and we won't settle for less than the best. One solitary change may not make a difference but when standards are raised all over then it 100% makes a difference. As each and every one of us began to raise our standards the culture spread throughout the club, and with it confidence rose and of course performance levels.

The place had been given a lift, we were encouraged to play football and not overly concern ourselves with mistakes made in trying to do so. The shackles were well and truly off. Prior to

Exeter we would play Plymouth, a huge game against a team who were in the dog fight with us. We won 2-0 and it was by far my most comfortable game of the season. By keeping the ball it meant the ball would change possession far less often and a result of that - it meant a much quieter game for the keeper.

Our bond had reached new heights.

A fresh approach and a different perception to our situation was exactly what we needed. Perception is a choice, one that is often shaped by what has happened previously. Foz and Warbo approached this opportunity with vigour and it was obvious that the cup was 'half full' again. The previous defeats were a distant memory and all down to a simple shift in perception of the very same situation.

Chapter 9 - February

"Points of view" - Power of Perception

Perhaps my most memorable game to date was playing (for Watford) in an FA Cup semi-final against Man United at Villa Park. The lead up to the game wasn't filled with the excitement that you may have expected. In fact I somewhat dreaded it. I remember being in Leicester at my headwear shop when the draw was made. My business partner and close friend Daren Duraidi was manning the shop while I was alone in the back room with a radio for company. With Ben Foster having joined us on loan from Manchester United that season it meant that he was ineligible to play if we were to be drawn against his 'parent' club. I spent most of the day thinking about the odds of us drawing Man Utd. It was unlikely. Being a semi-final it meant we had a one in three chance of drawing them - unlikely but possible.

The draw was made for us to play Manchester United, we were the first two names out of the hat and rather than jubilation I felt my heart drop. The game was a month away yet I felt instantly nervous. Why? The whole episode taught me a valuable lesson in perception and the power it possesses. I was focused on the enormity of the game, the millions of viewers this game would attract on TV and all I could think was of it going horribly wrong. What if I were to make a huge mistake in front of the millions watching?

Another big reason behind my nerves was that Ben Foster had played in the rounds prior to this game (except for one) and he was a standout hero in the quarter final win over Plymouth Argyle. He was the reason we were here and now that the big game comes he is unable to play. I'm already on the back foot before I even play the game, the self-doubt I had was crippling me but I didn't know it. My phone wouldn't stop beeping with loads of congratulatory messages, they had no idea.

Thankfully once the game came around I had reorganised my thoughts and my perception to be far more productive. I ran with the idea that this presented an opportunity to showcase my talent, a game that no one could take away from me whatever path my career would take, and something I would be hugely proud of in years to come. Another view I took is that although Ben had played the majority of the rounds leading up to this, I deserved this game, it was only a few years earlier that I had helped guide Watford to a semi-final against Liverpool (over two legs) only to break my cheek the week before. This was karma repaying me, Ben would get plenty more games such as this (three Carling Cup winners medals now to his name - I'm sure he's let this one go!).

I performed well in the game despite the defeat and truly believe that I only allowed myself the opportunity to play well by shifting my perception to a far more productive one. Perception is a choice and can be related to almost anything. I now choose a productive path where possible, one that will at least give me the chance to succeed. Success can't be guaranteed but putting yourself in the optimum mind-set to give yourself the best possible chance can guarantee that you have a shot and this is a choice.

Positive in defeat.

Wayne Rooney, a living legend.

On a similar note I often get asked if I was nervous before appearing on Dragons' Den for my headwear business (www.drcap.co.uk). The truth is that I wasn't at all. This, despite having only two hours sleep, after making the trip south from Morecambe, having played for Blackburn reserves the night before.

The Dr Cap store in Leicester.

My perception of Dragons' Den was that this wasn't the *be all and end all* for me. If we were successful then great, if not then at least we could take solace in what would be a fantastic experience and it would provide a story for years to come. That being said we ensured we prepared well, we wanted to be successful but I wouldn't lose sleep if we weren't. I have no doubt being prepared and relaxed helped in our pitch to the Dragons. I did have to load up on caffeine to keep me awake, six cups of coffee to be precise, but I enjoyed the experience.

It was only really after the show that I considered what might have happened had things not worked out - the Dragons can after all be quite ruthless. Before appearing on the show I hadn't even considered this train of thought. Apparently, ignorance can be bliss.

Next, Exeter and Ben Hamer

It was turning into a less than mediocre season on the league front as we found ourselves a few points away from the drop zone. The cups on the other hand had offered some light relief, the FA cup wasn't all that fruitful - bowing out tamely to Aldershot - but we made good ground in the League Cup. The best run that Brentford had achieved in many years, and now the potential of Wembley. A Wembley appearance was something of a rarity at Brentford and would certainly be the first appearance for me.

Exeter stood in our way; they were on a decent run of form and had rested key players in games prior to that night's game. We were on a dreadful run only halted by the defeat of Plymouth a few days earlier. We were underdogs for sure.

On a personal level I felt the nerves prior to this game. It had been a memorable personal run, for sure. In many ways it was the decision to *fight on* prior to our first round match against Stevenage that had offered me this opportunity. Making Wembley would be a fitting way to finish my first season as a Brentford Bee.

I kept reminding myself that I only have to make myself proud, give everything you can and control what is within your power. That is all you can do. I know that all external pressure and expectation is irrelevant but then the thought of all those fans who pay their hard earned money to come watch us play creeps into my head. I've felt guilty before, I don't want to let them down. I like to be liked. Most of us do.

Confidence in the unknown

Something I have personally struggled with is 'dealing with the unknown'. A game can throw up anything: situations I've never faced, I could get injured, sent off, make mistakes, and more.

These thoughts would make me feel uncomfortable. Each unknown scenario would put me in a situation that I wasn't comfortable with, the thought of which alone would cause me stress.

I now realise it's essential that you are 'okay' with the unknown. This isn't to say that you will be error free but you will play with more confidence and far less uncertainty. Simply focus on the game presented to you, and have faith that you have prepared the best way you could for every eventuality. If you do make a mistake then analyse and learn from it afterwards, *there is no such thing as failure*. This will help improve you further. To try and have control over that which is out of our control will lead to anxiety.

Linked closely to this is perception, which I have discussed earlier in the book. It's so important. Perception is a huge thing and anyone can allow themselves to go down a destructive path. This is a destructive path I've wandered down several times. Until the age of 21 I would regularly check online forums, that was until I read some comments not only slating my performance but the way I lived my life. I remember one comment in particular that stuck with me: 'Richard loves women, drink and himself'. This coming from someone I presume had never met me, and it bugged me at the time. I had given everything to my profession, a night out was a rarity and I was always very aware of my actions on a night out - knowing the pitfalls that were present.

I made a pledge then to never check forums again, which to this day I haven't (although my dad can't help himself!). With the world as it is now, with Twitter and Facebook in particular engulfing everything - you can't avoid all criticism. That's fine, my thought process has changed accordingly. Whereas a mistake used to be accompanied by guilt, I've since made a conscious decision to ensure that each mistake gives further motivation. Train harder, give more, don't let that particular mistake plague you. You are far too good for that. See it as a challenge, can you bounce back? What are you made of? For me this works, it gives me a buzz, it has nothing to do with anyone else, I like to be liked and admired but this is a challenge to me. All you can do is give everything you have, be wholly committed and be the very best you can be. Providing you do that then you will have contentment. External negativity won't penetrate if you don't allow it to, and in turn you become the master of your destiny.

"He who angers you, owns you."

To put focus and energy on something that is out of your control is time wasted. Accept the above statement and move on. When someone gives you mindless criticism, thank them for their insight and walk away.

Work Time

We were electric from the start of the second leg. Myles Weston and Sam Saunders were on fire, they appeared to have been given a new lease of life. Sam had been one of the few survivors of the previous era, forever the man to make way whenever things turned against us. Not anymore, he was well and truly a key player, his deliveries sublime, technically as good as any, and his work rate could never be questioned. Myles who was causing havoc on the left wing would supply the cross for Sam to open the scoring. Minutes later it would be two, Myles once again providing the cross for Gary Alexander to head home, giving Ben Hamer no chance. What a start!

It was like playing for a new team, not one struggling in League One but one full of confidence. We controlled the game from thereon out, and kept possession for large periods. Exeter's fans were frustrated, their players seemingly low on confidence, a psychoanalyst would have had a field day. On this form we could be champions, there was no doubt.

My goal was rarely threatened until the last minute when Exeter scored what would only be a consolation goal - but we were comfortably through. The final whistle blew, cue immense celebration, we've done it. I will get to play at Wembley at last.

The dressing room after the game was a great place to be, everyone bouncing around, the excitement levels through the roof "Wemberley, Wemberley!!...." An incredible night and the reality of stepping on the hallowed turf of our national stadium was beginning to sink in.

The Nike top was still going strong.

Such a buzz...

It begged the question, what had changed in the past week? The answer was simple to me, the mind-set of the squad had changed. No longer were we operating under an element of fear, we were free, 'express yourselves', a simple but powerful mind-set. We've all heard the saying that 'the pressure is off' and it really did feel as though it was off now. However it was only recently that I became aware that pressure is actually a choice. No one can make you feel under pressure, all pressure comes from within.

Pressure... what pressure?! - 'Pressure', the myth

Pressure is an internal creation, no one can put you under pressure, they can make suggestions but it's up to you whether you process their words in such a way as to make yourself feel under pressure, and experience the stress that accompanies it. It is your interpretation to decide to feel pressure. Much in the same way that no one can 'give' you confidence. This, once again, is an internal thing usually determined by perception of external events.

If you could do something incredibly well once upon a time and nothing has changed physically then you are still able to do that thing. It is only your mind that prohibits such an action. When players go through a rocky patch, quite simply they have an altered mind-set, often it may be thanks to a situation that had occurred, to which they have labelled a meaning. This in turn may have caused them to have doubts, and lose confidence. As a by-product of this the mind now questions something that previously required little or no thought. It can become a vicious cycle and lead to not only a downward spiral in form but severe self-doubt.

Having the awareness of this was a huge step for me. To be aware that a 'thought is only a thought', and it doesn't necessarily reflect reality is huge. Those not attuned to this will wait for something to help lift them from their slump. As a goalkeeper it may be a great save that helps lift confidence or a striker may score after a barren spell and feel back to his old self. Unfortunately, in today's game, this is no longer acceptable. By the time you've waited for this game changing event to happen you may already be languishing in the reserves.

The ability to have an instant reframe is so powerful, in fact it could mean that you never face disappointment again. Rather than getting stuck 'in' a problem and being one to tell the world about the situation you face, you are instantly searching for a solution to the problem, you refuse to be a victim of circumstance. Time spent elaborating on the problem itself is time wasted if you are not progressing towards solving it or if it means you lose focus. Problems and challenges are a part of life, the quicker you can move through problems the further you will progress.

Chapter 9 - February

You instantly adopt the mind-set that will help you bounce back to the top of your game and won't need an external event to help lift you there. Simply keep changing your approach and hold the belief things will improve, become very much of the 'glass half full' mentality. For me, adopting this method of thinking has been priceless.

Wembley was on the horizon, but due to the postponements of December we had nine games to play before our big day, and we were certainly not out of trouble. We sat on 35 points, and in most years 50 points would ensure safety. In an ideal world we would want to play the final with 50 points securely in the bag. It wouldn't mean much to win the cup but then get relegated. We set upon our task.

10

March
Timing is Everything

As we pursued safety, our first opponents were MK Dons and we gained a valuable away point which, in truth, could have been far better. We outplayed them and there was more than a sense of disappointment in the changing room at full time.

We would follow the Dons match with two victories; firstly a 2-1 victory over Tranmere Rovers and then a narrow win against Bristol Rovers. This game saw me face Will Hoskins who had been a team-mate at Watford only a year before. Will had always been a talented player but he had fallen out of favour early on at Watford. Bristol had certainly offered him a new lease of life; he was top scorer in the division for much of the season despite Bristol being destined for League Two football. This game became something of a personal duel between me and Will, one where I came out on top and in doing so earning another Man of the Match award. I now had a meal for 12 waiting for me on the back of my Man of the Match awards!

If only I had 11 friends…

We were on a roll and edging ever closer to the 50 point mark.

**I want to tell you this was a fantastic save... it wasn't.
Tranmere's equaliser.**

A stuttering performance over a 10 man Notts County would only yield a point and a disappointing display away to Hartlepool resulted in a 3-0 defeat; the first blip in what had otherwise been a faultless start for Foz and Warbo. 'Warbo', by the way, refers to Mark Warburton, it is something of a football cliché how a surname is shortened and the letter 'o' attached to the end of it. Even Simon Moore is referred to as 'Mooro', surely this is harder to say than 'Moore'? It has an extra syllable?! Fortunately my name doesn't offer the opportunity to do this so I'm happy to be referred to as 'Rich'.

"Focus on the present and the past will take care of itself."

In the Hartlepool match I was critical with myself for one of the goals as, although I had made the initial save, I could only parry it back out and it was followed up - resulting in a goal. No one else questioned me about this but I expect high standards from myself. A bad habit I had formed upon making an error was to spend the rest of the game thinking of a justification as to why I made that error, certainly taking me out of the present moment, and more often than not leading to further errors. Whatever happens, good or bad is instantly in the past and it's essential in order to be at my peak that I remain in the present. Quick reminder, what's done is done, focus. This provided another good challenge and I was pleased with how I played the remainder of the game.

Despite our defeat we were in a healthy position and only a matter of a few points from our port of call – safety. The sooner that mark was reached the more realistic a playoff push would become.

Oh and I was given an 8 for my performance against Hartlepool. It took a 3-0 drubbing in order to be awarded an 8 and make team of the week?! I'll take it although it only adds weight to my belief that many pundits lack goalkeeping knowledge. There is no way this performance surpassed the heights of Charlton, Everton or Birmingham.

I truly believe goalkeeping is a hugely misunderstood position. It is no longer a sought after position to play in the UK and I believe that this is due to several key aspects: firstly a lack of goalkeeping knowledge as a whole, secondly a lack of goalkeeping pundits needed to give a keeper's point of view, and finally the judgements keepers receive in the press from those who have never donned a pair of goalkeeping gloves.

Away from football I've set up a goalkeeping business (www.gkicon.com) aimed towards helping with the first of my points– goalkeeping education, and there was a significant spark that gave me the motivation to do this.

The team behind GK Icon.
(Richard Lee, Scott Loach, Alec Chamberlain, Ben Foster)

GK Icon was born

Let me explain how GK Icon came about. It was a couple of days after Steve McClaren's final game as manager of England, the 3-2 defeat to Croatia at Wembley and unfortunately a game that will be remembered for a Scott Carson error. Watching the game I could sympathise with Carson, conditions were terrible with torrential rain. The goal that he was lambasted for wasn't as bad a mistake as people will remember it to be. The ball was struck in such a way that it didn't rotate, significantly altering the flight of the ball (as opposed to when a ball has significant spin). It pitched just in front of him, zipped off the sodden turf and he was unable to get enough contact to turn it around the post.

Visibly there was a shift in his body language after this goal and despite coming back into the game England would lose and not qualify for the Euros. At the time Carson was a young lad, and was only playing his second game for England I believe. Things

Chapter 10 - March

had not gone to plan. I opened the newspaper, the next day, to see an article by Piers Morgan in which he annihilated the young goalkeeper.

It bugged me for so many reasons, but mainly because Morgan is held in high regard by many people. To this day I can't figure out what he contributes.

It's the easiest thing in the world to not do something and criticise those that put themselves on the line but fall short in hindsight, and this guy's writing articles and earning mega bucks on the back of that. How can this be right? Decision made. Goalkeeping knowledge is not where it should be, I'm going to make a positive impact on goalkeeping somehow. It was this moment that provided my spark.

A frustration I have endured in my life as a goalkeeper is: 'what height is considered optimum for a goalkeeper?' (which seems to be ever increasing). I've been branded too small on many an occasion, despite standing at 6ft. Now, do I believe I was born to be a goalkeeper? Perhaps not, the allergy I have to goalkeeping gloves suggests that this wasn't what was 'meant to be', unless as some twisted joke the powers that be thought it interesting to throw in another challenge, and ensure hands that crack when in contact with latex! It does however lead me nicely on to nature versus nurture. Are we 'born' to pursue something or is it a combination of coincidences, circumstances, and good timing?

My thoughts are this. I do believe genetics is important to an extent, for instance it would be tough to be a top flight goalkeeper if you were 5ft6. We are given certain attributes and some drawbacks but the important thing is that we are then granted a choice, do we aim to maximise whatever it is we have been given, or do we follow the path of blaming others for our inadequacies?

Those who succeed at a high level will look very different on the exterior, and have a variety of attributes they have tuned into (whatever it is they pursue) but the big similarity will come from how they have all programmed themselves - in a way that is conducive for success. I do believe we are all programmable, for want of a better word. We are fed a variety of content from thousands of different sources and we base our model of the world accordingly. By gaining an awareness of choice we can change this model in an instant and the results produced.

March Football

A tough run of games approached. First up Brighton, who were nailed on to win the division. If I were an 8 against Hartlepool then I wasn't far off a 10 against Brighton. Five minutes in and I produced another contender for save of the season, full stretch to my right from a close range header. I felt great, growing with confidence with each game, fully implementing all I had learned over the past couple of years.

Unfortunately a late own goal would mean a 1-0 defeat. This after yet another penalty save, the 17th of my career, from less than 150 games. Brighton had edged this game but not by much, we certainly weren't far from being a top team.

Proud to wear the GK Icon brand!

In saving the penalty I had felt a small pain in my left shoulder. I informed the physio after the game but I assured him it was nothing to worry about. I had actually had problems with this particular shoulder before which had resulted in a rupture to my left bicep so the pain was familiar. I stuck a bag of ice on it and didn't pay it too much thought. I wasn't training a great deal anyway with the number of games we were playing so it would just be a case of resting it between games allowing it the chance to heal.

We would get our just rewards away at Charlton on the Saturday. I made an important save low to my right in the second half which would prove crucial with Leon Legge grabbing a last minute winner. This was perhaps my favourite save of the season, it was certainly the most flamboyant, low to my right I saved it on the half volley and scooped it out in a similar fashion to that of Gordon Banks. Okay, maybe not quite in the same league as *the* Gordon Banks save but it's certainly the closest I've come!

This would take us to 46 points, one more win prior to Wembley and we could play the game without any threat of relegation looming, it really was a solid run we were on, and the football was of a high standard.

Sunday Swim

Sunday swimming sessions soon became a regular theme under the new regime, the idea being that this would reduce lactic acid build up and be of huge benefit if we were to have to play again on a Tuesday. This wasn't the most popular addition to our regime but it was understood. At our regular Sunday swim sessions we would often encounter the same people enjoying their Sunday in the pool and Jacuzzi, while we did our exercises in the pool.

One lady in particular always caught my attention. She would be in the pool, normally dressed in shorts and a t-shirt. She had somehow mastered the art of moving all her limbs without moving, yet floating, sometimes even finding herself drifting backwards. I honestly thought she was drowning when I first saw her. The thing that really intrigued me wasn't her swimming technique though, it was that when she did finally make it to the other end of the pool she would pause briefly, take a deep breath and would proceed to execute the tumble turn with pin point precision. Was she just mocking all of us?

Another tough test at Huddersfield next, a 1-0 defeat in the last minute. Tough to take but again huge strides were being taken and the feeling around the place was bubbly. We were part of a progressive organisation with Wembley on the horizon. During this game I was forced into a save high to my left, the pain in my

Chapter 10 - March

shoulder was there again, it wasn't improving but again I wasn't concerned, this shoulder's been troublesome for years. The summer wasn't too far away, I'd have plenty of time to rest then.

Next up would be an in form Leyton Orient - a club record 16 games without defeat leading up to their game with us. We were also in good form despite losing three of the previous four if that makes sense?! We were playing football that deserved more, the fans appreciated that too. This is often the case, supporters can accept defeat providing we are giving them something to enjoy, we were doing this now.

We started the game on fire and were two up early on.

I was enjoying a relatively quiet game until the stroke of half time; the ball broke to the right hand side of the box, eight yards out. Using my trusted technique of closing the ball down - attack with chest, spread arms at 30-45 degree angle, legs slightly turned and fully tensed all over to ensure maximum chance of making contact with the ball.

I got there quickly. He opted for power. I spread instantly, the ball hit my left arm and cannoned to safety, great save but then instant agony. This wasn't right at all, my arm felt as though it was detached from my body, this wasn't normal and the pain was excruciating.

I rolled over and felt a pop and the pain eased ever so slightly. I knew it had dislocated but thankfully soon after slipped back into its socket. The pain was intense but more prominent in my mind was the Wembley date only two weeks away. I knew instantly that I was as good as ruled out. I haven't cried for a long time but I was crying now and it had nothing to do with the physical pain. In this moment I questioned my belief in karma.

I couldn't move my arm and made way for Si Moore.

Wembley in doubt.

Neil Greig, the now first team physio, took me to the hospital less than a mile from the ground. An x-ray revealed no break but Neil told me that on average it would take 8 weeks for a recovery and being a goalkeeper that time could be more than doubled. I was devastated.

The lads won the game 2-1, Si pulled out a cracking save to his top left hand corner to ensure victory and end Orient's run. Although that evening I was feeling distraught I was delighted for Si. He's on course for a fantastic career and it honestly couldn't happen to a more genuine lad.

Si Moore would face competition for the Wembley game from loanee Trevor Carson, acquired from Sunderland for a month. Coincidentally Leyton Orient would go on to lose several games in a short space of time after our game - confidence is a funny thing, incredibly powerful.

Chapter 10 - March

I woke up the next morning, still in pain but with a refreshed mind-set. Enough feeling sorry for myself, time to reassess my goals, reframe the position I'm in and get on with it. Firstly I needed to know if I'd require an operation. With Neil Greig for company we visited a specialist shoulder surgeon.

The surgeon said I would be best off trying to do rehabilitation work first, before opting for an operation, so next I wanted to know if it was definitely impossible for me to play the final. I was informed that the usual healing time for a dislocated shoulder is around 8 weeks as Neil had told me, although commonly closer to 12 weeks for goalkeepers.

I questioned the situation, why is it a 12 week program? What if I work harder than anyone else has done with this injury, could I return in 3 weeks? Perhaps not but why not try? What have I got to lose? I had already been ruled out of the remainder of the season so there was absolutely no expectation.

After getting over the initial acute pain attached with an injury of this nature I told Neil of my intention: 'I will play in the Wembley final'.

Prior to this I had considered Neil's likely response. Let's imagine I did play and got injured - this could reflect very badly on him. I could imagine him walking me off the pitch and it being the longest of his life! With everyone questioning why a top class physio would allow someone to play within two weeks of a dislocation?!

I decided not to focus on this scenario; this certainly wouldn't have helped in reassuring him we could do this. I then put to him the idea that I play to a high standard, we win, and in doing so stretch the boundaries of what is conventionally believed to be fact.

I had offered him an outcome goal that suited both of us and thankfully he was motivated by the prospect. We set out a daily plan - process goals each day, this was our 4 minute mile! My focus was pure, I was open to every form of treatment offered, I had hypnotherapy sessions, daily sessions in an oxygen chamber, prolotherapy injections to aid healing, three hours worth of shoulder work every day followed by swimming, a high protein diet, 8 hours+ sleep every night. Long story short I explored every angle I was aware of, and some that had only recently entered my awareness.

10 days later and we revisited the surgeon to get his thoughts. He examined me; we ran through a series of tests, we sat down. He got out the scans that he had read a week previously. He used the words 'car crash' when referring to the scans but he went on to say that the strength and movement I was showing was more like someone who is 8 weeks into rehab as opposed to 10 days. He gave me the 'okay' to play. It was only 7 days before this that I had developed a rash under my arm where I was unable to muster up the strength to prise my arm away from my side without piercing pain.

Neil was fantastic and backed me all the way, he explained that it had never been done but he knew that I wouldn't accept this suggestion as the truth; I would simply say 'this hasn't ever been done *yet*'.

I kept it quiet from everyone other than Neil and my coach Simon Royce but I was making rapid progress. 10 days post injury and I trained secretly with Roycie, I got through it okay. It wasn't perfect by any means but I was committed, I wanted to play this game. The reason I had decided to keep it quiet was that I felt I had nothing to gain by telling the world I was going to play. If anything this could lead to embarrassment on my part and take focus off the team.

I then trained more intensely the next day, which was the Thursday before our big date on the Sunday. I felt good and was due to meet with Foz and Warbo the following morning to signal my intent.

Chapter 10 - March

It was that evening that my mind-set altered for the first time and I had huge doubts. In going to retrieve an item from my car I felt my shoulder slip, it was still loose and the feeling was not only painful but made me feel quite nauseous.

I started to question myself. Am I 100%? No, at best 80%. Do I feel confident in diving full stretch to my left? Not really. What would a re-dislocation mean? Probably surgery, which potentially could mean forced retirement.

Then the thought that delivered the knockout blow. This final wasn't about me. To play when not fully fit would be unfair when someone of Simon's calibre would be more capable given the circumstances. We had also won the two games I had already missed, I needed to benefit the team, not hinder it. My perception had shifted and now my reasons 'why' not to play were far outweighing my reasons to play.

I met the manager and explained the happenings of the night before. We agreed that if I was able to come through training unscathed then we would sit down and talk later that day. I barely lasted 10 minutes, a shot low to my left I saved well but there was that sharp pain again. I hadn't dislocated my shoulder again but I wasn't right. I had made huge steps but this one would evade me. Disappointment for the second time over the same injury. Refocus, reframe and go again.

I haven't exactly had the best time over my career with injuries. In particular, a ruptured bicep, torn meniscus, cheek bone broken in two places, eye socket broken in two places, severe concussion, broken humerus bone requiring 4 screws and now a dislocated shoulder. Each one a severe test but in hindsight each one has offered valuable lessons. With each one I owe a huge debt of gratitude to the talented physios who have helped rebuild me along the way! I knew that under the guidance of Neil Greig my shoulder would recover and I would be back. The efforts he had put in already were above and beyond anything I could have asked for and for that I was truly grateful.

It begins…

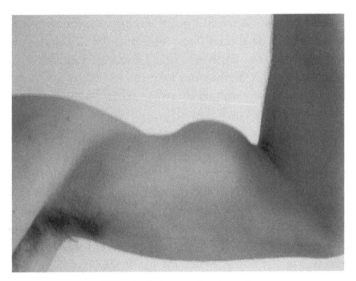

The infamous 'unicep'.

Chapter 10 - March

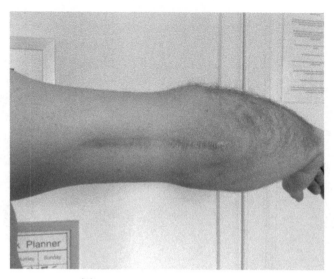

The scars of a goalkeeper.

I received many notes when I got the injury, via Facebook and Twitter, many along similar lines: 'you must be devastated, we are so sorry for you'. The truth was that I recovered quickly emotionally. I had reframed and taken stock of my position, and where I had been a matter of months earlier. I actually felt fortunate - as strange as it sounds.

My view was simply this - had I dislocated my shoulder in one of the reserve games I played earlier in the season it would have gone unnoticed and understandably so. I had come to Brentford and set my goals out from the off and I was thankful I was able to exhibit what had helped me play at the highest level and equally thankful for the open minds of the Brentford faithful. First impressions can last a lifetime. Not here. I was forgiven and embraced. I felt at home, hence my gratitude.

I had never cared much for football previously but the fantastic support I had received over the season certainly helped me see the game in a different light.

With all this in mind I thought it appropriate to give my thoughts which I did via my personal website www.RichardLeeGK.com.

22 March 2011

Richard Lee out of JPT Wembley Final

Ok, so I guess most of you are aware by now that the news isn't particularly good and for what it's worth I'd like to share a few of my thoughts. I'm obviously frustrated with the situation, I knew instantly that I had dislocated it and in that moment that my Wembley hopes were unlikely. I did spend a day or two feeling sorry for myself but I've come to terms with it now and am feeling very positive about things. The truth is that this season has been the most enjoyable of my life, if perhaps the most turbulent!

If someone were to tell me that I would have 3 keepers play before I were to be given a chance to show what I could do, to then be involved in cup wins against Hull and Everton (and what should have been another scalp against the eventual winners Birmingham!), enjoy huge wins at Charlton, Southampton and Exeter amongst others, not to mention saving the odd penalty here and there on the road to Wembley, I wouldn't have believed them but I would have taken it in an instant.

What I guess I'm trying to say is that although I am so grateful for the hundreds of messages of support I have received in the past few days (and they really have cheered me up believe me, I am so thankful) I'm feeling positive about all of this now. I have had my fair share of ups and downs, which is part and parcel of the life of a footballer and I'm prepared for the next step. I will find out the exact extent of what I need to do to get me back to the form I've showed this season and go beyond it, and I will do whatever I need to do to make that a reality.

I, along with every Brentford fan I'm sure, am excited for not only the promise of Wembley, but the ever improving football that we are playing with a very talented bunch of lads under the guidance of Foz and Warbs. I'm really excited for what the future holds and have no doubt this will only be a minor speed bump in the bigger picture.

To finish I would just like to give a quick mention about Simon Moore. For those who are unaware of Simon, I have had the pleasure of working alongside him this season, he is a fantastic keeper and if he is to get his chance then I could think of no one better to do so. He has all the attributes needed to make it to the very top and with the guidance of Simon Royce, who I'm indebted too hugely for playing such a major role in my personal progress this season, he has every chance of doing that.

Thanks again for your support, it really is appreciated.

Regards

Rich

11

April
Mind Coach

The big day arrived. April 3rd, and for many of the lads – the big chance to play at Wembley beckoned. The JPT is a strange competition in that, to begin with, it isn't taken all that seriously by many clubs - most would rather put their focus on league form rather than an extended JPT run. We had negotiated the earlier rounds whilst resting players but as the competition progressed and the opportunity to play at Wembley grew ever more realistic, we took this very seriously. How many people can say they've played at Wembley, regardless of why? Today would be a first for many of our lads.

For the past few days I had assumed the role of 'mind coach' for Si Moore, he had edged out Trevor for a starting spot. A huge occasion for anyone but bear in mind this was only his fourth professional appearance and a crowd of 40,000+ was expected. I wanted to do whatever I could to ensure he controlled his nerves appropriately to give him the best chance of performing well. I kept feeding him positive messages and he was spot on. Despite what would be a disappointing final, ending in a 1-0 defeat, he came out with praise, making one particularly good save early on. I was delighted for him, he had grown in stature throughout the season and now not only did he have a Wembley appearance under his belt, he also got the opportunity to rack up some league games until the end of the season at least.

Si Moore – 'Destined for greatness'.

The Wembley experience was obviously not what I'd hoped it would be, however I found enjoyment in the day and could certainly appreciate what an incredible arena Wembley is. It fuelled the motivation inside me to want to play here before I'm done.

The coach was a quiet place on the short drive back to Brentford, the excitement over the past few weeks had well and truly faded. We still had an outside shot at the play offs but there would be no JPT winners medal this season.

I had bought a large number of tickets for this game, with many friends and family looking forward to seeing me play at Wembley. Most had decided against coming when informed that I wouldn't play. Someone who did come however was someone who had played a huge role in mentoring me over the past season: Bob Patmore.

Bob Patmore

The book 'The Celestine Prophecy' speaks of coincidence and the law of attraction. Quite a spiritual book but I like the idea that you attract into your life what you give out. Maybe that would be the explanation for what I thought to be a quite random meeting with a guy called Bob Patmore.

The story goes a bit like this, I was on a night out with friends. On the night I would be introduced to a friend of a friend, and after a short discussion I was told I must meet her friend - he offered a great pension for footballers. Now why I decided to attend this meeting with this guy as opposed to the hundreds of other financial agents hovering around football is still unclear to me but we arranged to meet. The guy's name is Bob and I typed the address into my sat nav. Dressed in my usual attire of jeans, flip flops and t-shirt I arrived at quite possibly the most stunning house I had ever seen. This guy must arrange a lot of pensions!

It turned out that a financial company was one of his many dimensions, he was also a footballer in his younger years as well as being involved in the music industry. But more interestingly to me, he was involved in personal development. We bonded instantly sharing many similar ideas in regard to beliefs and values. I knew instantly Bob would be a great influence on me and he has been. Throughout the season we would meet regularly and discuss ideas. Having several businesses of my own

I instantly saw Bob as something of a role model, he had implemented his ideas and they had provided him with a fantastic life.

Now I'm well aware that having money doesn't elevate you above others in any form. To me though, I have respect for those who have dedicated themselves to a noble pursuit and have put together processes that have enabled them to earn a large income and enjoy the kind of life that most of us dream of. Bob backed up many of my beliefs, he had a very similar belief system to my own and in doing so had achieved some incredible things in his life, and is still doing so now. In choosing a role model it is essential they are worthy. Bob was more than worthy and I'm very grateful to now consider him a friend as well a mentor.

Not only was Bob the inspiration behind me writing this book but he was also part of the inspiration behind my latest business venture that I have set up (for more information check out www.everyoneneedsamentor.com). Born from the idea that we can all benefit from someone who has already experienced the path we wish to pursue.

Be a sponge

'You become your peers'. Once in a group the natural thing to do is move with those people in the group. It can be uncomfortable to see someone break away to bigger and better things and it's nice to 'fit in'. This isn't necessarily a bad thing and I would say that I was fortunate in choosing a group of friends who are also progressing with their chosen pursuits and who also share a similar positivity about their future.

Having grown up together we do share a similar model of the world but in order to continue my learning it's important that I continue to meet people who are succeeding in areas where I am not currently, but wish to, and to soak up the wisdom they offer. The truth is that they've succeeded where I haven't, yet.

Therefore they know something I don't. Now rather than brand them lucky or allow my ego to convince me otherwise I will happily open my mind to what they have to offer, ask good questions to aid myself and allow further growth.

I wouldn't class myself as a naturally good public speaker, I would however like to have the ability to own a stage so I will find people that can offer me what I need in order to be a worthy speaker. Many who have succeeded will be more than happy to share that information. I sincerely get a thrill when some advice I have given to a young keeper pays dividends; the email of thanks after a good performance brings a great feeling, the ability to give is far more rewarding than to receive.

My friends

Another nugget of wisdom I received from the book 'The Celestine Prophecy' was in regards to those who give energy and those who steal it, the scenario given was somewhat mythical but it contained a powerful message. In basic terms to me it meant that it would be far more beneficial to hang around with positive giving people than negative 'poor me' people.

This was something I was naturally aware of growing up. Why would I want negative people around me, people telling me that I can't do something or that I wasn't good enough to do something?! I choose not to associate with the type of person who will drain the energy from a room, who not only believes the glass is half empty but doesn't even like what's in the glass.

It was actually a close friend of mine, Graham Abbott, who taught me this lesson almost by accident. We went to secondary school together and we spent a lot of time together outside of school too. The details of the day itself are a blur but during a quiet moment I decided to tell him that "I was tired", a rather innocuous comment and one that other people have said to me regularly. But Graham questioned *why* I had told him that, and I had no answer.

Why did I tell him that? Who cares that I'm tired? How is this piece of information going to add to our day? The majority of the nation is tired but by telling him this I'm not only bringing down the room ever so slightly, I'm also convincing myself - this message will embed itself into my subconscious.

Despite this comment I would consider myself and my peers as positive, giving people; we all share a belief that life has incredible opportunities on offer and we aim to seek them. I'm attracted to people with a positive mind-set, the idea that anything is possible and the excitement that accompanies that thought. Perhaps I was fortunate initially but I'm now very aware of who I choose to spend my valuable time with.

New role

I would do a lot of work with Simon over the coming weeks: phone conversations discussing mental processes and helping to guide him through potentially destructive thought patterns. Breaking down limiting beliefs became my role for the remainder of the season. It was something I gained huge satisfaction from. I've spent years studying performance and to have the opportunity to help others achieve their goals and reach new levels gave me an immense buzz. Perhaps I've found my calling when my career is over?

Something we spoke of regularly was that of finding Simon's 'Optimum Performance State'.

First discussed in Chapter 2, we all have an 'Optimum Performance State'. This can vary between sportsmen, some perform at their best when truly relaxed whereas others need to feel nerves in order to reach their optimum levels. There is no right or wrong. This was something I had never really considered, I just accepted that for some games I would feel good and for other games I may feel lethargic. Some games I wouldn't be all that nervous, whilst with other games I would be emotionally drained before the game had even begun. OPS is more commonly known as the inverted 'U'.

This can be controlled and much of this comes back to awareness of thought. In simple terms the ultimate goal is to play a match at your peak, feeling energetic, alert and confident. The things you do prior to a game will have an impact on this. Now, you could feel incredible and have a poor game or feel terrible and have a good game but the idea is that over the course of a season/career the more often you feel pumped for a game with confidence and concentration levels high, then the more successful your career will be. Simple. To discover what your ideal performance state is and to have the ability to replicate it again and again will help go a long way towards being successful in whatever you do.

Recovery

I met again with the manager early the following week and we agreed that taking a long term view, and to give myself the best chance of a full recovery, we would put a line through the season. I would spend the remainder of the season building up the power in my shoulder. I had come so close to playing in the final but this made sense with regards to my future. The shoulder was still weak, it may never be as good as it was but by ensuring all the muscles surrounding it are strong there is no reason why it can't be very secure and more than capable of withstanding the rigorous training of a professional footballer.

I set new goals, got myself in the gym, and set upon my task. I'm aware that a shoulder dislocation for a goalkeeper can be career ending, the fact that I will be diving with my shoulder in full extension as well as lunging in head first to oncoming attackers does put the shoulder at more of a risk than for an outfield player and with each dislocation a shoulder will get weaker and weaker before needing a less than guaranteed operation.

However I wasn't overly concerned by this, maybe this has something to do with me not being scared about life after football if this were to happen, but I think it's more to do with the thought that I know I'll be okay regardless. This thought process actually brings an element of freedom with it. I'm confident that I am *more than my career* and I know that whatever happens to me - I will deal with it. What is the worst that could possibly happen?

Dr Pepper mentality

I love the Dr Pepper adverts and their famous slogan 'what's the worst that can happen?!' and this applies to so many situations. Okay, so I play a game of football and play a bad game. My ego will be slightly dented, maybe I'll feel some embarrassment, maybe I'll get some criticism but I will recover from all of that and I will find ways to recover in a more efficient way each time it happens. The alternative is to hide away, live in that comfort zone which although (as the name suggests) is comfortable, it's also a frustrating place to be. Seeing the world around you progress while you refuse to advance, with the worry of the unknown.

A memory I have is that of being at the end of year school dance as a teenager surrounded by lots of pretty girls, many of whom I'd have loved to have spoken to but I just wouldn't. I would spend the majority of the night thinking of reasons why it wasn't a wise thing to do with every different 'what if' scenario running through my head and ending the night with a feeling of disappointment in myself. What is the worst that would have happened? Okay she may have rejected me and some of the lads at school may have ridiculed me but these would have been lads of a similar mentality to me at that time, subconsciously we were all holding each other back, no one dared break away. I learnt that it's far easier not to do, and criticise those that do, but inevitably this approach will never lead to fulfilment. It's those people that 'just do it' (maybe I should call it the Nike mentality?!) who succeed, (well unless you are Piers Morgan apparently). And with each so called 'failure' a lesson can be gained to help propel life forwards. Simply put, with each girl that would have turned me down that night I could have found a new way of *what doesn't work* with girls! I certainly would have been more enlightened.

Interestingly enough once the Wembley game had passed, my recovery speed slowed considerably. I worked hard on my rehab work but I didn't have a motivational goal as powerful as Wembley in mind anymore. The plan now was to ensure that I didn't rush things and my body reacted accordingly. Having been told I had two weeks to recover, my mind and body did everything in its power to make that a reality. I now had 12 weeks to recover, once again the mind and body will work in unison to make that a reality.

The season would somewhat peter out in a slightly disappointing fashion. A home defeat to the doomed Swindon would banish any playoff aspirations and the last month became something of a non-entity. This may have cost Foz the chance of getting the job full time.

I had a lot of time for Foz. Having the decency to call me after I dislocated my shoulder was a nice touch, thanking me for my efforts goes a long way with a player and I have no doubt his name will crop up again in time.

Blog IV

Running Down The Clock (October 2008)

As the game against Preston was drawing to a close, we held the ball in the far corner of the field, using a common method of running out time - a random thought entered my head and one that has been in my mind a lot this week.

I personally don't agree with the current method used to time football and I'll tell you my adaptation which I believe will enhance the game.

Put quite simply, I believe we should play to a stop-clock, every time the ball leaves the field of play the clock would be stopped and restarted the instant it re-enters play.

Ninety minutes would be too long if this was the case so I would suggest a 50-minute game (25 minutes each way). I say 50 minutes as this is the average time the ball is in play in a typical Championship game.

The idea wouldn't change the game too much as all games would kick off at 3pm and the majority would finish around 4.45pm as is the case now.

The big difference would be that there would be no argument as to how much added time there should be or complaints of time-wasting/cheating. A lot of the current methods used to run out time would still be used, i.e. holding the ball in the corner but with a much more accurate method. No longer would players go down feigning injury or players take exceedingly long over each dead ball situation because it would be an irrelevance.

It confuses me slightly that two games can be played, one where the ball is in play for 65 minutes and the next where it's in play for 45 minutes, surely that can't be right?

Imagine the excitement as your team holds a 1-0 lead and there are 30 seconds left on the clock, knowing that your team just needs to keep the ball in play for a few more seconds without error. Or alternatively another scenario of a team scoring with only a few seconds left on the clock, imagine the elation/dejection.

I can't imagine this would take too much effort to introduce; I am though fully aware that having 90-minute games is tradition so the likelihood of this actually happening is, at best, unlikely in the foreseeable future.

Admittedly, I do watch a lot of American sports which is a big reason as to why I'm swaying towards the way of a stop-clock. I'm sure we've all seen footage of Michael Jordan sinking a basket in the final seconds to claim a victory and seeing the arena erupt, it's thrilling.

It may be a case that this set-up is only possible in the top couple of leagues to begin with as I couldn't imagine Sunday league teams or even teams in the lower leagues being able to afford the technology needed to create this. (Although a stop watch could suffice).

I have no doubt that this idea has been suggested before and I'd be fascinated to know the reasons it was rejected, or the 90 minute game seen as preferable.

Chapter 11 - April

For now, when leading, I will continue to take slightly longer for each goal kick I take, knowing that each second the ball is out of play is still very valuable.

12

May
Positive Reflection

An exciting 4-4 draw away to Huddersfield would bring the season to a close. A season that would see us finish in 11th position, accumulating 61 points in the process. On the face of it this wasn't an extraordinary season at all, a mid-table finish coupled with a defeat in the JPT final probably won't go down in the Brentford history books as being overly significant but on a personal level this season eclipsed all others for a variety of reasons.

The challenges I had experienced over the season stretched me in ways I had never been stretched before. Finding myself as third choice keeper within a matter of weeks of arriving at Griffin Park, and finding a way to fight my way back, and in doing so playing some of the most memorable games of my life, helped not only back up the set of beliefs I have instilled in me but will certainly live long in the memory. Inevitably I missed out on the showpiece finale but I like the view that this was my final test. I didn't need that game anymore, I had graduated.

The methodology

I realise I'm not a household name to most but I see myself as a living case study of sorts. There are many who can spout the theory without ever having put it into practice, I've read most of their books! But I know that I wasn't 'naturally' confident as a kid, my mind-set had contradictions that I needed to understand before I could excel. I've read more books than I care to think of and I've 'stuck in there' when I could easily have opted out.

I've written about many situations that I've faced this season in particular and the ways in which I've tackled them. I do have a certain methodology behind how I operate and what has brought me success over the past couple of years in my various pursuits. It's been developed over years of reading, attending seminars, feeding off worthy mentors and in gaining a qualification, but in essence my methodology when broken down is quite simple. It is a methodology that allows me to deal with any situation in a productive way and often comes back to the following key points.

- Set goals, process and outcome
    - o Have a sense of direction in which you are heading.
- Find a powerful reason why
    - o Something that motivates in such a way that you know you will do whatever it takes to find a way to succeed.
- Control what is within your power
    - o This is all you can do. To try and control that which you have no way of controlling will lead to frustration. Realise what elements you can maximise and be content in doing that.
- The ability to 'reframe' situations quickly

- o Find the most productive path and run with it, being stuck 'in' a problem won't help solve anything, choose your perception.
- Live in the present
  - o Give everything to the present and the past will take care of itself. You can't affect what has already happened, however by focusing on the here and now you give yourself a far better chance of maximising each moment, each situation, and creating an exciting future.
- Eradicate excuses, take responsibility
  - o We can all make excuses but this won't improve us, if you could've done better then realise it, accept it and rather than try and talk your way out of it, take steps to ensure that you improve next time.
- A thought is only a thought, it doesn't necessarily reflect reality
  - o You can choose your thoughts and beliefs. Just because someone has a belief about you doesn't mean you have to choose to take on that belief; learn to guide your thoughts in such a way to provide a platform for success.
- Continual and never ending improvement (Kaizen!)
  - o A nice idea to run with, the idea that you will commit yourself to 'continual and never ending improvement' and believe me when I say you'll like the changes that occur.
- Any perceived pressure is internal, you have the ability to alter this
  - o No one can put you under pressure. With a heightened awareness of thought you can choose how you feel in any situation, choose the state to best suit you.
- Thoughts release chemicals, be aware of your thought processes
  - o Think negatively and you will experience unpleasant emotions, alter your thought pattern to help release much more pleasant chemicals into the body and the natural high that comes with it. You can change your thought pattern whenever you choose, circumstance need not affect us, this is our choice.

Chapter 12 - May

- Choose empowering beliefs
    - Beliefs are generally formed on past experience, however we can change any belief we wish to change. If you realise that a belief about something is holding you back – a limiting belief - then you can change it to whatever you wish. Beliefs aren't 'facts'.
- Powerful physiology
    - Physiology can play a huge role in your own thoughts, feelings and emotions. The simple action of sticking your chest out can make you feel better about yourself, so when feeling down arguably the first port of call would be to improve your physiology.
- Appreciate other's 'model of the world'
    - Most of us will believe that our way is the right way, however we all have a different idea about what the right way is. To appreciate how others see the world can give us an advantage when communicating with them.
- Flexibility in approach
    - Have a goal but know there are many ways to reach that goal. If something doesn't work then change your approach, flexibility is key.
- Anchoring states
    - Learn to anchor positive states, have the ability to call upon useful states when needed and in doing so enjoy the benefit to performance.
- Quality of questions
    - Gain awareness over your questions, do they offer a productive outcome? If not then why ask them?
- Improve communication
    - To others and yourself. Why choose negative self-talk? Why doubt yourself? We all have the ability to empower ourselves by choosing our communication wisely. Again, this IS A CHOICE.

The fact is this: nothing is guaranteed. There is no formula to *guarantee* success. However by following basic rules there is a way in which you can open yourself up to possibilities.

The methodology certainly won't guarantee that I will play the remainder of my career error free, it's simply a process that I enter into, knowing that with each setback there's always a positive alternative to whatever uncomfortable situation I find myself dealing with, and doing it in positive manner.

If someone's mind-set is uneducated then it will stand more chance of pressing the self-destruct button or giving up on a pursuit as opposed to finding the route which will soon lead to good things once more.

"This too shall pass."

Chapter 12 - May

My new philosophy is quite simple: the realisation that you *can* demand from yourself and that is the *only pressure* you ever need to live up to. People will criticise me of course, they will criticise and I may not perform to my best week after week - but I can always give myself the best opportunity to do so by approaching games with the same excitement I had as an 8 year old making my first ever penalty save, with the chance that every game I play provides the opportunity to be a hero for a day.

There are more intricate details but this is a fantastic foundation for peak performance. There is no 'right' or 'wrong' in how you should pursue your goal but these rules will mean you are in a productive state more often than not, and in turn allow yourself the best opportunity of attaining whatever it is you desire.

Some of this may not be natural at first and as with anything it may take time to fully adopt some of the ideas given. Even when fully grasped it's still something that is a continual process but one that will, over time, become something you do unconsciously (stage 4 - unconscious competence). I had a quote hanging up in my room as a kid that I didn't fully appreciate until learning what I have and that quote was this:

'Act the way you want to become and you will become the way you act.'

Choose your mind-set and in doing so choose your own path, before you do anything you must have a process that will allow you to achieve it.

My last and biggest lesson - Enjoyment

If we agree that the sense of enjoyment is simply a manifestation of our thoughts then it can be agreed that enjoyment is a choice. With this in mind it occurred to me that a traffic jam would be far more enjoyable if I were to release the worries of being late and what may or may not lie ahead on my arrival and instead focus my mind elsewhere. I turned the music up, felt the sun coming through the window and allowed my thoughts to drift in the line of exciting dreams I have for the future (whilst concentrating on the road of course!).

This situation happened to me towards the end of the season and it was quite liberating. I had left home with plenty of time to spare but what would normally have been a 30 minute journey turned into a 3 hour journey. I was helpless, I wouldn't have done anything differently in hindsight. I had no regrets, so why worry about what may or may not be said to me when I arrive? I'll deal with that then, for now I will enjoy the moment and I really did, a pleasant state engulfed my body as I sat stationary on the M4 heading in the wrong direction. If I can enjoy this, I thought, then I can enjoy anything!

With this in mind I refer back to my comments I made earlier in relation to not enjoying football. It's true, for the majority of my career I have disliked the game - the injuries, the chronic nerves, the intense scrutiny and the criticism endured making it something I have been keen to escape from for some time.

However it was during the 2010/2011 season that I made a truly life changing choice and it was perhaps the simplest decision I had made in my life.

I chose to enjoy football.

The things I detested previously are still present but they are now an irrelevance when focusing on the thousands of great things football can offer. I am finally at peace with who I am and where I'm heading, and I know I'll deal with whatever life can throw at me.

Graduation.

I claimed all five player of the season awards. Justification. Goal achieved. Enjoy the moment, reframe and refocus. Let's go again.

The end.

Appendix A
Q&As from the Website

Over the years, various excellent questions have been posted on my website. I'd like to share a selection of them with readers and any aspiring goalkeepers here.

Mind-set questions

Posted by James Hunter

Q. Hey Richard, firstly don't hate me because I'm a Reading Fan! I have a 15 year old brother who is a goalkeeper and he played in a youth cup final last week, the game went to penalties and he missed the last one meaning his team lost. He's gutted and was really upset. Is there any particular way we can lift him? Thanks.

A. Sorry to hear that but also delighted to hear that. The reason I say that is because it's when we come up against some form of adversity that we are able to grow as people and improve ourselves.

It is a shame that they lost their final but I'm sure there will be loads more opportunities in the future and there are plenty of lessons to be taken from the experience. The fact he put himself up to take a penalty takes a lot of bottle and I'd like to think that when the situation comes again he'll take one again and it could be a very different outcome.

There is a quote somewhere along the lines of the harder you fall the higher you bounce back up. Basically I've always found that, in my career, my best time has come after getting a setback. It's great when things are going well but in many cases it takes some form of pain to give you the kick to improve further.

Your brother will be fine, you can't win every match but it will give him a lot of confidence to come through this and feel stronger for it.

Posted by Dom

Q. Hello Richard, I was just wondering what books you got about the mind-set?

A. Ok here's a few good ones I've read lately

- The Monk who sold his Ferrari - Robin Sharma
- Guide to Greatness - Robin Sharma
- Tackling life - Jonny Wilkinson
- Awaken the Giant within - Anthony Robbins

These all have elements that can be applied to football but more ideas about how you can live your life how you so choose, I found them all interesting in different ways and selected bits from each that have helped with my goals.

Posted by Renaldo Sutherland

Q. Hi Richard, I am a Goalkeeper wanting to make it pro but find it hard to push into that area. I feel that I am just under, trying to progress as I play semi-professional, and also play for my county. How would you go about getting professional in this situation?

Another question is that I've had trials for a lot of professional clubs but I feel I crumble under the pressure and do not play as well as if I were with my friends at a game (a more relaxed environment). What did you do when you first had your trial at Watford? What was your mind-set for playing well, which in turn helped you join Watford and become a great professional? I would love to play at any standard in professional football and need to know what I have to do to become a pro, my dream, and soon England's number 1 keeper!!! Thanks :)

A. An area that I believe is massive for a goalkeeper is mental training and mental awareness. Now I wasn't born with this but I feel I've improved it. I read a lot of books on psychology and having the right mind-set. I actually came up with a paragraph that I read prior to a game that although very simple has taken me a while to come up with and accept, it is the following:

'Prepare the best you possibly can, train hard, eat well, sleep well, live well. Approach each and every game with an inner conviction that you will succeed, give the game all you have, this is all you can do and you must have peace with that'.

By me having this mind-set I am at ease with myself, which I believe has taken me years to achieve although I still get setbacks from time to time. In fact I had one earlier this season regarding confidence but by remembering that all bad things that happen are presented to us to teach us a lesson means we don't have to beat ourselves up.

For whatever reason bad things will happen so use them as a positive. Find the lesson within the setback. It's great that you

have a dream, keep reminding yourself of that and use it to help motivate you. This is your 'reason why'.

I've advised a few people on how to get pro clubs to recognise them so I'd ask you read through the answers I gave to them but in short I always encourage people to make things happen. Don't be scared of rejection. I would challenge you to embrace it even! Even if 99 clubs don't give you a trial but one does then it was worth it, and when you get that trial enjoy every minute of it, and just know in your heart that you gave it everything you've got.

Posted by Michael Duffy

Q. Hi Rich, I think you're doing really well so far. I am a goalkeeper who plays for an under 13's side and I'm a bit worried to tell players to get to the back and front post. What do you do?

A. Thanks! :-) . . I remember when I was young and I had a similar problem with telling team mates what they should be doing. With age I've come to realise that when you are playing football you need to be quite forceful. If you want them to cover the posts you need to tell them because you are in charge back there. They may not want to do it but if it stops a goal then they'll all be thanking you later. It's also important to remember that instructions on a football pitch aren't to be taken personally; we all like to win and in order to do so we must be assertive in what we say to each other at times.

Game Related Questions

Posted by Noel McCoy

Q. Hello Richie. Just looking for a basic pre match warm up to use before my games. Also, what are your thoughts on the new sells wraps? Lastly, do you play any other sports to improve your goalkeeping like badminton or tennis?

A. Warm ups are quite personal, basically I would recommend doing whatever it takes to feel 100% for the game. For me it's a mix of handling drills, crossing drills, and distribution drills. I only do a few repetitions of each so not to tire myself for the game.

I've always been a fan of Sells wraps, not sure if I've tried his latest ones but I have no intention of using anything else in the near future. They do have great grip in all conditions.

Regarding other sports, I used to play loads, I found basketball in particular was great for my goalkeeping and tennis was great for footwork. I don't really get chance to play many other sports now, well except for golf - but that doesn't really help my goalkeeping!

Posted by Luke

Q. Hi Richard! I'm 16 and I believe I am a good goalkeeper. However my greatest weakness is taking dead ball kicks. I just can't do it. My defenders keep having to take them and it's really embarrassing for me. Could you offer your advice on how to improve? Thanks!

A. Kicking really is quite a personal thing and my advice is always quite simple, go out with a mate or two and whilst having a chat just clip balls to each other, mess around with your technique, see what feels good, curl the ball different ways, try drilling it low, then clipping it high etc. You'll soon find a technique that works for you, once you have this technique then work at it, practice regularly, and keep improving it.

Start taking your own goal kicks and challenge yourself, how many times can I hit the centre forward? You might start by hitting him 3 times out of 20, but by the 5th game you hit him 6 times out of 20. Gradually improve game by game. Start small, gradually build up and in doing so you'll notice that your confidence levels rise. Keep telling yourself 'I am a great striker of a dead ball' and soon enough you'll improve, and take your kicking and all-round game to new levels.

Posted by Ben Daniels

Q. Hi Richard, I am a goalkeeper and I was just wondering if you have any tips on diving. I have no problem diving high and low to my left but I struggle diving to my right because I can't take off right and then struggle on the landing technique, and I always manage to land on my ribs and it hurts. So if you have any tips I would be pleased to hear them. Thanks Ben.

A. Most keepers have a favourite side (I'm no exception). My advice would be to break down the dive, so start doing drills on your knees and work on falling to your right and getting the technique correct and comfortable.

Then progress to using a crash mat (if possible!). This can be an excellent way to work on throwing yourself to either side with no danger of injury and can also help with increasing the power in your legs. A drill I would do is to start with the ball in my hands and pretend the ball is heading for the top corner and I would literally throw myself as far as I could and really focus on landing softly and keeping hold of the ball - a little bit unorthodox maybe but it has certainly had a very positive impact on my career to date.

Other simple exercises for power would be to do simple squats; keep a straight back and feel the burn in your thighs as you lower yourself down and up repeatedly. Like anything, good practice makes permanent. Before you know it you'll be hurling yourself through the air and plucking the ball from the top corner

Posted by Brad Simpson

Q. Hi Richard, I was just wondering how to improve my catching skills so I get "softer hands" because I may be getting a trial with Ipswich and I want to be able to catch better than I do currently. My goalkeeper coach says I snatch at the ball sometimes. Are there any drills I can do to help with this? Thanks a lot and best of luck for your season.

A. It is natural at a young age to 'snatch' at the ball, obviously you are eager to get hold of it so don't worry about doing this. I guess my best bit of advice would be to trust your hands. Get your technique right and trust that the ball will stick.

A very simple drill that I've done all my life and which used to drive my family crazy is to just lie on my back and throw and ball up and down towards the ceiling and catch it on the way down, each time concentrating on cushioning the ball in and getting the perfect 'W'. I would then progress to throwing it up, move my hands down by my waist and return them in time to catch the ball, basically copying what happens in a match situation. Just get used to catching a ball repetitively, it really does help with ball familiarity.

Posted by Simon Doherty

Q. Hi Richard I was just wondering:

1. Should a goalkeeper use strapping tape around his wrists or fingers during a match/training and would you do it yourself?

2. What equipment should a keeper take with him during a match or what should he bring/use in training?

3. What are the best gloves to use? I have been using Sells last season and this one and they are doing me no harm!

4. Do you have any tips on kicking or what I could do to improve kick outs?

Appendix A

Thanks, Simon.

A. Ok here goes.....

1. I personally don't use strappings. My belief is that, by using strapping, your body gets used to them so could weaken a particular area (just my belief I must stress). I do, however, use strappings if I have a problem in that area, for instance after twisting an ankle or spraining a wrist etc. We are fortunate in that we have physiotherapists to do the strappings, plus they are qualified in doing them in the most efficient way.

2. For training I'd always take a large bottle of water with me, when dehydrated you risk injury and poor performance. I'd also wear padding if the ground is firm, elbow and hip padding mainly, not for games though. Obviously for games I'd wear shin pads, I wouldn't wear these for training unless we were playing games in training - then I'd put them on. A towel is always useful if conditions are wet and a cap can be handy if the sun is bright.

3. I personally wear Sells so would of course recommend them! They are being worn by a lot of top keepers now which is proof of how good they are I believe.

4. Kicking is largely to do with technique. My advice is always to just practice different techniques and find one that works for you. The way I improved most when I was younger was to go to the park with a mate and spend the day clipping balls to each other, trying various techniques to do so. You'll soon find out what works for you.

Hope that helps

Posted by Harry

Q. Hi Richard, I am at Crystal Palace and being coached by Colin Barnes. When he was your coach, what was the most important thing that he told you about dealing with crosses, shot stopping, pass backs and communication?

A. Ok in order...

Crosses - positive in decision making, decide whether to punch or catch? Deal with it at the highest possible point and do so with good spring and whilst 'attacking' the ball.

Shot stopping - On your toes, always expect a shot, eyes firmly on the ball, ready to explode, always look to catch and if not possible then parry into a good area.

Pass backs – Have you got time to take two touches or does it have to be one touch? Make an early decision, if one touch then ensure a solid strike, get your weight through the ball. If two touches, then take a good touch and pick out your target.

Communication - Clear and concise, don't commentate, just the important information that the defender needs (Away, man on, push up, etc)

I would also add a few things to that list. I believe your body language is important, look dominant and if you do make a mistake (which we all do) then react well, make sure your next involvement is a good one. I actually have a list similar to this which I refer to before games to make sure I'm switched on to my individual tasks. Hope this helps. Say hi to Colin for me, he's a fantastic coach!

Other areas of your game

Posted by Tom Boyle

Q. Hello Richard, I'm a 19 year old goalkeeper who is currently playing at semi-pro level, I have ambitions to play to the highest level that I can. What advice would you give me to carry on improving my game? I see you mention Yoga, how does that help you? Cheers mate; any reply would be gratefully received.

A. Well you have the most important attribute going for you and that is your willingness to learn and to want to improve. As basic as it sounds as long as you commit yourself to that then you will fulfil what potential you have for sure.

The different aspects I'd look into would be first and foremost the mental side of the game, what can you do to make you feel 100% for every game and play with a confidence/arrogance that no one will beat you. You need a very secure mind-set to be a top keeper and that's something that I believe can be developed over time and certainly can be learnt by reading the right books and getting appropriate mind coaching etc.

Yoga is very good as flexibility is essential to play at the top level. Another aspect is power, when I was younger I downloaded some basketball programs from the internet and adapted some of the spring exercises to improve my game and it helped me a lot, a lot of focus placed on improving the strength in your thighs in particular, this is something you could do.

Lastly technique is vital, they say practice makes perfect, I prefer the idea that perfect practice makes perfect. Model your game on the best goalkeepers in the world, set your targets as high as that and you'll accomplish things far greater than you'd have ever imagined.

Posted by Tamsin

Q. Do you have a special diet crafted for you each day, and a high carb one before games? I know the Arsenal players all have to sit down and have a meal together after matches - do you guys have to do this?

A. We are taught the benefits of nutrition and have a pre match meal together although not after the match. Players are responsible for their own well-being but most players do follow a schedule of carb loading prior to a game in order to feel at their peak during a game.

Another important factor which I find very important is hydration. I heard some fact that something like 90% of the population in this country are dehydrated and the impact for a player on performance can be seriously damaging. It affects energy levels and concentration which are two major factors to a player's performance.

I believe there is still room for improvement in the area of nutrition though and I think we'll see further strides in the coming years that mean players really are playing at their absolute maximum week in week out

Posted by Gaz Williams

Q. Richard, like yourself I'm not the biggest keeper around (I'm about 5'10) but I'm currently playing at a decent standard, so I was wondering if you do any special plyometric exercises in the gym or out on the training pitch to improve your spring? Thanks Gaz

A. Yeah plyometric exercises in the gym have been great for me. I was told a formula a few years back - Strength x Flexibility = Power. So basically if you can build up your leg strength (Squats being a great exercise) and combine it with some plyometric work then you'll see great results. I often do the following session for spring:

Squats x 8 using heavy weight - fast feet for 10 seconds - 8 drop jumps.

I would repeat this series 4 times followed by stretching (very important). A drop jump is simply having two low level benches next to each other and dropping from one box and rebounding onto the other, ensuring that you have minimal time on the ground.

There are many drills you can do to help spring and to be honest I devised most of mine from basketball programs I found on the internet! So use your imagination, see what drills you find and set up a program for yourself. Test yourself now on how high you can spring, perform a program for a month and test yourself again. I was delighted when I did this and I saw a big increase in committing to it.

Posted by Kev

Q. Hi Richard, I am just wanting a bit of advice on pre-season training. What does your pre-season consist of, and have you any tips for what I should be doing. I am 19 and any advice would be great thanks mate.

A. Ok, a goalkeeper's pre-season. Well my personal opinion is that a goalkeeper doesn't need to be able to run 5 miles, that isn't part of our game, we need to be fit but in a different way. We are required to be powerful, explosive etc.

So my advice would be to do goalkeeping drills but at a higher intensity than normal in order to get a level of fitness required to play in goal. Combining that with gym work, strength training and plyometric work will be far more beneficial that running for hours on end.

I also do yoga from time to time. I know Brad Freidel swears by this, it's great for flexibility and also for calming the mind, I would recommend it.

My advice in general would be, if you enjoy it then open yourself up to soaking up all the info you can. Watch top keepers perform, study their techniques and create your own unique personality in goal, enjoy improving and see where it takes you :)

Posted by Matthew

Q. Hi Richard, as you've set up a goalkeeping school, does this mean that you're looking at becoming a goalkeeping coach after you've retired? I know retirement is still a long way off, but do you have any thoughts of what the future may hold?

A. I have a long term plan for myself, which at my age will be a combination of playing and coaching side by side (injury permitting).

I honestly believe that I have some ideas that could help revolutionise goalkeeping in England. I will look to put emphasis on areas of the game that until now haven't had the time dedicated to them that I believe they deserve.

I have a keeper in mind, a keeper that I want to help create. It is the keeper that I strive to be and will continue striving to be but I realise my time in the game won't last forever and I know that coaching will be the next step for me and I will help to create some of the very best keepers. I have no doubt.

Posted by Charlie Mills

Q. Hi Richard I was just wondering how do you know when you should go and collect the ball from a cross? Also I wanted to ask you the best tips that you got to be a good goalkeeper, I would love to hear them because I want to be a successful goalkeeper just like you. Thank you so much

A. Regarding crossing, I would say your starting position is vital, try to be really positive with it, don't leave the goal open but the further you can be from your goal once the cross is taken the more chance you have to come and get it. With crossing try to be positive with your decisions, defenders love a keeper who will come and collect crosses on a regular basis.

My biggest advice is always the same, love to learn. That doesn't just apply to football either, whatever your pursuit may be - it is such a great attribute to want to learn and better yourself and is very rewarding. Many who are successful in life will adopt this approach, be flexible and open to new ideas. Model your game on the very best and set high standards for yourself. Be your own harshest critic in order to give yourself areas to find that extra 1%. At first your friends and family might give you some stick for the changes you have made but the results will be rewarded and if you apply this to football then your game will reach new heights!

Posted by Tamsin

Q. You've said previously that your training sessions aren't that long, do many of the players stay on and do extra training or do you generally just do the group training and that's it? Do you think you should be doing more training in order to reach a higher league? And do you do much strategic work, like analysis of the opposition and tactic talks?

A. Technical training sessions aren't all that long but then it's up to the individual whether he wants to do extra. Most of us do some form of extra training and yeah you will get a few lads practising free kicks and other techniques after training.

The coaches are wary not to overdo the training because although not long, the sessions are intense and the main goal of a training session is to make sure the players are in the right frame of mind and feeling 100% for the upcoming game. So, doing more training it's not always necessarily beneficial. I like the idea of training 'smart' and not necessarily to the point of exhaustion. Performing techniques poorly will if anything have a detrimental impact on performance.

And regarding your other question, yes we get a document every week with info on the opposition, it will include individual information as well as team information. We also do quite a bit of work on our team shape and set pieces during training. This will usually be done towards the end of the week as it's not quite as taxing as some of the training. Then lastly, on the day of a game, we are shown clips of the opposition so that we know what to expect.

Thanks for your question.

Posted by Rob Zand

Q. Hi Richard, firstly great website! Secondly, I was wondering what exercises you do in the gym, upper and lower body? And finally do you take any supplements in order to help with building strength, power? E.g. protein shakes, Thanks, Rob.

A. Thanks Rob, yeah I do take protein shakes twice a day when doing my weights program. I'll usually have the shake along with strawberries, blueberries, raspberries, bananas, pineapple, etc. I'll have one first thing as it's a great way to start a day and maybe one before bed. Maximuscle is quite expensive but it has been proven to help with muscle recovery and muscle building.

Regarding what I do in the gym, I focus a lot on basic exercises such as squats followed by some form of plyometric program. It's a basic theory but the stronger your legs are then the higher you'll be able to jump, and the more power you'll have in your kicks etc.

I'll also do calf raises, hamstring curls and quad extensions, again all to condition the legs, each exercise using heavy weights with low reps and keeping a note of my progress.

For upper body I'll do the bench press followed by an exercise for the back. Shoulder Press is a good exercise and I'll always do plenty of core work: sit ups, planks etc. Bicep curl and Tricep curl are also useful for general conditioning.

It's important to know why you are doing the weights, my belief is simply that strength is a great thing providing it doesn't hinder flexibility or speed. I've seen keepers who get too big and struggle to move because of it. I would highly recommend doing a Yoga course alongside your weights to give you that balance.

Appendix A

Height Issues

Posted by Bart

Q. Hello Richard, My lad has just finished his first season at a Championship club. He is the only Keeper signed at his age group (under 14 for next season) although many have been on trial. He has done well and gets plenty of praise. Have heard a whisper that he is being tipped to be one of the five lads they think, at the moment, should make it to scholar stage. But with him, it's been said "so long as he keeps growing". He's not short by any means, he's 13 and 3 months old and stands 5`6ish". He`s quick, sharp, very good hands and as brave as you like. Which makes me laugh when we play other sides whose keepers are 6'+(at 13!!!!) but who are slow, not very sharp and bad handling but "fill the goal". Personally I think he will be as tall as me (6 foot) but this even seems not big enough these days. The club recently released their under 16 who was about 6 foot and signed a 6'5" guy released by a premiership club, and this lad was decent. It would seem that the chairman and the manager want a big keeper, which doesn't bode well for my lad in 3 years' time. (that's assuming he's good enough) It does make me laugh, have these people not seen Casillas, Valdes and the likes of your good self play? Would the likes of Banks, Shilton, Bonnetti and Clemence have been signed when they were 16? Sorry, starting to rant lol. So, my question is, in your years as a schoolboy at Watford was your stature ever mentioned to you as a stumbling block.

A. Ok you've basically just put across my argument to every manager that I've ever played for! You are spot on, for whatever reason a lot of English coaches see size as such a big deal and it's an issue I've come across several times, I am 6ft on the dot but as you say even this is viewed as being 'small' for a goalkeeper.

I think if you have the size and the power/technique to match with it then that's great, I had the pleasure of working with Ben Foster and credit to him, he's got the lot but there's nothing more frustrating for me that to see the big lumbering keeper stood in goal with the half the ability of the lad who is his understudy due to being four inches smaller and by the way those four inches equate to zero once you take into account positioning, decision making, spring and quickness etc.

I guess my biggest bit of advice would be to do whatever you can to not make this an issue, I'm sure you and your son will have many discussions about this in years to come if he keeps progressing but try not to dwell on it.

One thing I've learnt in my time is to not allow anyone else to take 'power' away from you. So the idea being that those who constantly make excuses for where they see themselves have given away the power and have lost focus on where they wish to be. They now have no control over where they stand because 'it's not their fault'.

Now as much as the height issue can frustrate, I know in a funny way it's irrelevant. If I continue to do what I know I can potentially do then I'll continue to be offered contracts and will have a successful career in the game. The second I start blaming my stature is the second my game will suffer. There is a lot to be said for being very positive in your mind set, even to the point of arrogance. Just know that height isn't an issue and have supreme confidence in your ability to save the day for your team etc. There are examples of 'smaller' keepers succeeding at a high level in the UK, continue to focus on these examples and keep striving for the stars!

I wish you and your son all the best.

Big Decisions

Posted by Confused Mum

Q. Hi Richard, My 8 year old son has been "spotted" & asked to go for a summer trial at (another) local club. Given the time

Appendix A

commitment (travel) / knock on effect on siblings / & high chance of it all ending in disappointment for my son, I'm not keen. But my husband thinks we'd be mad to pass it up. I feel my son's still very young - do you think if I say "no" now he won't be eligible for a chance again in a couple of years? Confused Mum.

A. Hi confused mum!

I fully understand your dilemma, my situation is that I have 3 younger brothers, so as a 10 year old joining Watford and having to make the 60 mile round trip 3 times a week it was quite a strain on my mum and dad and one that I didn't appreciate until I was much older. But it is one that now I am truly thankful for.

Now what you say is true, if you look at percentages then as good as your son is - the chances are it will end in disappointment. But what if it didn't?? My guess is that your son's biggest dream is to be a professional footballer right??

This has definitely been my toughest question this week as I know it's easy for me to advise that he should go but I do realise it would be a massive commitment for you and it isn't quite as simple as that.

I guess I just look at my situation and think if I were sat in an office right now doing something I had zero interest in then would I be happy? The honest answer is no. Thanks to my parents I have been allowed to follow my dream and because of that it has helped me achieve personal goals I would otherwise only have dreamed of. And even if the whole thing had ended in disappointment then at least I would've known I'd given it a shot and no doubt grown from the experience rather than being that frustrated guy in the office, going to the pub on a Friday telling everyone how I could've been something.

If there's a way you can help make it happen then regardless of the outcome I know your son will be very grateful in years to come.

I hope I haven't made you more confused!

Posted by Pierce

Q. Hi Richard, I am a 16 year old who has recently just found a passion for centre back. Although it doesn't have much to do with goalkeeping I have been told I'm better at the back than my previous position of centre midfield. I have been told by my coach I have good tackling and reading of the game. So I was wondering... is 16 too late to get picked up by a club? Also I live in a remote area which doesn't help. I just badly want to make it into the game. I eat healthy and hit the gym to gain strength, at what age did you join your first ever club?

A. I was young but that's very unusual these days, most of the lads I play with now didn't join a club until they were 15 or 16, so it definitely isn't too late. My biggest advice to those looking for a club is simply - if you think you are good enough then let people know.

Although the fairy-tale story is that you are playing for your Sunday league club and there's some mysterious scout in the crowd who spots you and signs you up, this unfortunately isn't really the reality. It certainly wasn't for me. In fact, our Sunday league manager at the time told the Watford scout to come watch us play and we ended up winning 10-0. I didn't touch the ball, it was only down to the recommendation of my manager to the scout that I got a trial, so had it not been for him pushing me I probably wouldn't be in the position I am today. But it did teach me a lesson in that you can certainly make things happen for yourself if you have a passion for something which you undoubtedly do.

So write letters or get some quality video footage together, whatever it takes to best advertise yourself then make things happen and refuse to take no for an answer and absorb all advice given along the way. You live once, make the most! :)

Appendix A

Good luck.

Posted by Keiran Harris

Q. Hi Richard I'm 16, very enthusiastic and passionate about football. I'm the youngest player for both of my teams. In one of my teams (apart from me) 18 is the youngest and on the other 21 is the youngest - so I'm used to playing with people much older than me. Most of my friends and team mates say I have what it takes to play at a high standard, I train as much as I can and I am considering going for trials at places such as Sutton and other teams at that level and would just like to know what sort of training do midfielders at Watford do in training? Also any ideas what sort of stuff can I do on my own? Thank you.

A. Well firstly it sounds like you are doing the right thing in terms of testing yourself. The higher the level of players you are able to train with the better you will become as they will stretch you and test you.

The sort of thing you could do on your own, which most of the outfield lads do at Watford is to spend plenty of time in the gym. The way the game is now the stronger you are the more effective you will be.

I'd also ask you to assess what weaknesses you believe you have and make an effort to work on them, spend time in the park on your own or with mates. Focus on technique, on your touch or your passing. Decide what sort of a player you are and make yourself the most effective player you can possibly be.

I think you are doing the right thing in getting trials at non-league teams to begin with, but don't be disheartened if you don't get signed straight away, football is a game of opinions and if you are good enough it will happen sooner or later.

Random Questions

Posted by John Howes

Q. Cheers Richard for the gloves you gave me at Carrow Road you are a nice bloke it was a pleasure to meet you. I keep asking about boots, do you wear a size too small?

A. No worries. Yeah I guess I technically do wear a size too small, then I wear them in the bath to stretch them to mould to my feet. I've done this since a young age as I like a tight fitting boot, this is just what I do though. I wouldn't recommend it as my toes are now quite badly out of shape!!

Posted by Janet Walker

Q. Hi Richard I was just wondering what actually happens on a match day, like what time you have to get the Stadium?

A. Here's the script:

11.45am - report

12.00pm - pre match meal

1.00pm - team meeting (discuss tactics, watch opposition clips)

2.15pm - warm up

2.45pm - finish warm up

3.00pm - kick off

4.50pm - 3 points in the bag :)

Posted by Tommy W

Q. Hello Richard Over Xmas I was seeing some friends and we bought FIFA pro 08 for the Wii. The first game was Watford versus Luton with a certain Lee as my goalkeeper. Imagine my surprise as Mr Lee wandered 20 yards out of goal and promptly got lobbed resulting in a 1-0 defeat (I admit I had not read the instructions at this point, but I still had to pay for the pizza). Do you ever have any say in having your name used for these things? I notice that the character also had a bit of beard too. Can I have the money for the pizza too please?? :-)

A. Ha, sounds like you are as bad as me at that game. In fact the lads have a screen set up at the back of the team coach to play that game and pro evolution on long away trips, although they are very rarely Watford, Normally Barcelona or Man Utd, no idea why?! ;)

To be honest we don't get any say, I'm assuming it has something to do with the league holding the rights to using our names for these games and I know certain games don't have the rights so use names that are almost correct, I'm sure you know the type.

I hope you got revenge for your defeat to Luton, just shows how unrealistic those games are eh?! And as for the pizza, I'll be sure to send the money in the post... ☺

Personal Questions

Posted by Richard Walker

Q. Who is your idol?

A. Iker Casillas, he's a similar age to me and he's played for Real Madrid regularly since the age of 17. He's the most talented keeper I've ever seen and someone I aspire to even now.

Posted by Richard Walker

Q. Was there a time during your arm injury that you thought you might not play again?

A. In truth that was never a consideration. I had managed to break the humerus bone, which is the bone in your upper arm, a very unusual injury.

I was told post-injury that it was career threatening but I knew it wouldn't empower me to think like that - by retaining a positive attitude I believe it helped me through that time.

It was a tough time though, as I remember the doctor telling me I'd never be able to straighten my arm and, had that been the case, then my career would most certainly have been over. I remember spending countless hours leaning up against a wall trying to straighten it and the result was that although I've been left with a large scar on my right arm, I can near enough straighten it and I've had no problems since.

Appendix B
Q&As with the Pros

Scott Loach (Watford FC)

What age did you start playing in goal? Did you ever play outfield?

I've always been in goal, since the age of seven.

Did you ever play outfield?

I did for a little while before that - I was very young so not properly, really. So ever since I've been seven, I've been a goalkeeper.

How did you get spotted? And who was it for?

I first played for Ipswich Town from the age of 8 until I was 12 because I used to live down there. My family moved down from Nottingham. I'm not too sure how I got spotted to be honest. I was just playing for my local team and then when we moved back up to Nottingham, I just carried on playing locally, and then ended up at Lincoln. It just went from there, really.

Why did you want to be a goalkeeper?

I used to love Man United and Peter Schmeichel was my favourite player so I just wanted to follow in his footsteps, really.

Why was Peter Schmeichel your idol?

I just thought he had everything, and he was like a hero back in the day, so I just looked up to him massively.

Was there anyone in your life who was particularly influential?

My dad was a big influence on me because he played non–league football as a goalkeeper and every kid looks up to their dad. He's the one who used to look after me and stuff like that. My dad was massive, but then as far as players go I just loved football in general and Man United was my team. Schmeichel was massive for me.

How did you do in school? Do you have any advice on education for young keepers?

Yes I was fine in school, I just worked hard. When I was in school I worked on my school work, when I was out of school I worked on my football. I didn't try to mix up the two and think I had made it. I didn't let my school work bother my football, you concentrate on what you are doing at that moment in time. It's just one of those things - if you put your effort into it then everything will go well.

What has been your greatest football-related experience?

Probably playing for my country at Wembley for the Under-21s.

What's your best ever save and why?

I played Tottenham in the Carling Cup and I made a save from Aaron Lennon to my right and pulled it out of the top corner – it was probably my first real big save I made for Watford and it was against a big team live on television. So it is one that will always stick with me.

What is your mindset prior to games? Do you get nervous? How do you deal with it?

I don't get nervous to be honest, I look forward to every game. I get really excited. I'm really excited now about pre–season starting. I love playing and I've got my music to listen to before a game. I've got a set play list so I get myself focused by doing that.

Do you analyse your performance after the game?

Every Monday or Tuesday depending on if we've got a mid-week game I sit down with the goalie coach Alec Chamberlain and he'll have all my clips ready from the game and we'll spend twenty minutes to half an hour going through them. You see where you've went wrong, you see what you did right, and it's just little things, just little inches that help you go further.

How do you deal with mistakes? Does it ruin your weekend?

No, I just forget about them. Mistakes are going to happen and I feel that I've got a strong mentality and I'm going to make mistakes all through my career. I would like not to but you've just got to deal with them. Just make sure you make the next stage and bounce back.

Do you think about and watch football in your spare time?

Yes, always. I've watched nearly every game in the World Cup and try to look at other goalkeepers to see what I need to be.

Do you enjoy football as much as you did when you were younger?

Yes I still love it.

Are there days you dislike football? Have you ever been close to quitting the game?

No, never.

What's the worst injury you've ever had? Was it hard to come back?

I ripped my stomach muscle off my hip bone from diving. The physios looked after me really well and I was back within eight weeks but it was the worst pain I've ever had – it hurt when I breathed and coughed for a good two weeks but once that was out of the way it was easily mendable.

Did you doubt yourself at all through this experience?

No, I was confident in my own healing process and the people that were around me. The physios were great with me and I know the structure at Watford was great. I was always confident I'd get back in good nick.

Is nutrition important to you?

Yes, massively. I'm quite a big guy anyway so I need to eat the right food so that I fuel my body. It's important I eat a lot of food but make sure that it's the right food.

Do you do much in terms of strength training and plyometrics?

I do a lot of strength training three to four times a week, sometimes more if there is only one game. It's something I enjoy so I do a little bit more and it's not something that I feel that I have to do. It's something I enjoy doing and get the benefit from.

How often do you practice distribution?

Probably three times a week.

How important do you think distribution is in the modern game?

Yes massively. As a goalkeeper you have to kick the ball every day in training so you get to work on your technique there. But there are actual set routines. You do actually work on your distribution everyday if you concentrate properly. I think it's massive in the game now – you can be first line of attack from time to time.

Do you think it's essential to be tall to be a keeper in the modern game?

Yes I do. There are a lot more big players - it makes you a lot more dominating but then there are people that can prove that height doesn't matter. You've got Rich (Lee), you've got Iker (Casillas), you've got people like that, who are not the biggest but have had great careers and not let it affect them. So I think it helps and depends on if the manager fancies you to be honest.

Do you believe your talents were a product of genetics or through hard work? Or both?

I think a mixture to be honest. I've had a lot of hard work, and then my size and my frame that came through family genes. So a bit of a mixture.

What is your biggest motivation?

Just the buzz of walking out on that pitch every Saturday afternoon. The moment you walk out you have such a big buzz and I don't want that to stop.

What advice do you have for up and coming keepers?

Keep working on the basics, just work hard and keep listening – you can never master anything even if it is handling or kicking, and if you think you're good at them all - just keep doing it. Repeat your training, and just become really solid and consistent.

Ben Hamer (Charlton FC)

What age did you start playing in goal?

I started playing in goal at the very early age of five. My mum and dad moved out to Germany when I was about three or four as my dad worked for the MOD, so the early part of my life was spent out there growing up.

My dad took me along to a training session at a local football team and obviously I was quite new to the language and had to kind of adapt the language to speak the language. I went to this training session and we all gathered up and got some games going and they said 'who wants to go in goal?'. I think everybody put their hands up so, like a sheep, I put my hand up as well, not really knowing what was going on. I ended up getting stuck between the sticks and I think it stayed from there. From then on I was a goalkeeper.

How did you get spotted?

First of all I started off with a trial at Aston Villa at the age of nine. When we moved back from Germany we lived in Bristol and after a year I was playing for a local team. Aston Villa is not near Bristol but I got invited to a trial and went up to their training ground at Bodymoor Heath I think.

I had a trial game and played very well. A week later, we played Tranmere and it was a bit of a weird one: their keeper got injured after about ten minutes and I was supposed to share a couple of halves with one of the other trialist goalkeepers. I ended up going in goal for Tranmere for a half. It was a bit of a strange experience because I actually wanted Villa to win so I didn't really play well. Obviously, a week later, I got a letter saying they wouldn't be taking me on so it was a bit of a lesson learnt to always play well, and not to take a gamble.

Who was your idol and why?

I think in my time it was Peter Schmeichel and David Seaman. David was obviously the England keeper at the time so I looked up to him. With Schmeichel, a lot of goalkeepers growing up around my time would say him: playing for Manchester United, one of the biggest clubs in the world, and he was just one of those guys to look up to, a massive presence in the goal and a fantastic keeper.

Obviously on the England front, David Seaman was a leading goalkeeper, a rock. I watched him during Euro 96 when he saved a couple of penalties against Scotland I think, and started following him.

Was there anyone in your life who was particularly influential?

Obviously my dad and my mum were great influences on me. They used to ferry me around, as I used to travel on Tuesday nights and Fridays for training. They used to make the journey which was a two-hour journey up there (so it was a four-hour round trip) just for training, and my step dad as well. It is not even your own son but he was doing four-hour round trip car journeys so I can get to do my stuff. So I owe a lot to them.

How did you do in school? Do you have any advice on education for young keepers?

I think school is very important. When I was at school I was a terror really for the first few years but then I kind of settled down and realised it is important to learn and have a good education behind you. I always wanted to be a footballer and when people asked me at school what I wanted to be, I would say footballer and they would laugh and say 'no what are you really going to do?'. From then on I started to think maybe that is a lesson to learn, if it doesn't work out then you need something to fall back on and in the last couple of years of school, I got my head down, worked hard and listened.

I think it is important in life to listen to people more experienced than you and you can learn valuable lessons off them. That was the stage in life where I took that on board. I passed all my GCSEs and got Cs and above, except for Maths which was a very poor subject on my behalf. Apart from that, I got good results and got a scholarship to join Reading and went to do that for two years.

What has been your greatest football-related experience?

I went on loan to Brentford from Reading for a season and we won the league that year. I played every single game that season and got promotion at the end of the season so that was a very good year for me. Last year wasn't a great year as I found myself number two for the whole season. But I did come on in the FA Cup game against Liverpool, who we overcame over two games. I came on in the second half after our keeper went off injured, and played against the likes of Steven Gerrard and Fernando Torres, which is something you want to do every week and strive to do.

What's your best ever save and why?

That is a hard one really, which one to pick. Obviously when I played the whole season at Brentford I made a few important saves in important matches. We played against someone like Dagenham, which wasn't the most fashionable game in the world but I pulled one out of the top corner, going backwards. It was a looping shot from outside the box and I managed to pluck it out of the top corner. So that is probably one of the saves that sticks in my mind but hopefully I will do some more saves on the bigger stage further on in my career.

What is your mind-set prior to games? Do you get nervous? How do you deal with it?

When I was younger that was a big negative of my game. I used to get really nervous and get worked up before games. I used to worry about things going wrong and stuff like that but it was something that I did eradicate.

You need to have a confidence or an arrogance when you go out there and if you are a nervous person when you go out there, I don't think it helps. I can have a positive effect. Of course nerves, they can help, but they can hinder you as well. When I go out on a Saturday then I am normally quite confident as I have rehearsed what I am going to do in the games, the situations that can arise, and take them on board.

It is important to have an arrogance about you on the pitch. I don't tend to get nervous any more, the only time I get nervous is when my family and friends are there in numbers watching, and I want to do well in front of them. Then I do put a bit of pressure on myself but apart from that, I am not really a nervous person.

Do you analyse your performance after the game?

Yes, I think it would be wrong if I didn't. I look back on the things I could have done better and the things I did well to use as positives. It is an important tool to have to reflect on the game you have just been through. Look at it in the next week at training and try and eradicate things that you have done wrong or where you can improve. I think it is a massive thing to reflect on games you have just played in.

How do you deal with mistakes? Does it ruin your weekend?

I think it is fair to say it does. Obviously every goalkeeper hates making mistakes but it is a big part of the game which inevitably happens which you can't really get away from. Sometimes you will be concentrating to the maximum and something out of your control can go wrong and it obviously is down to you. Your mistake can cost a goal or cost the game. If things like that happen to me I will stew over it for about a day or two but then I don't let it affect me after that. If I have a game midweek then it is gone by Monday. I have training, I forget about it and get on with my work.

It is important in games that if you do make a mistake then you need to forget about it and make sure the next thing you do is spot on and right, and then it breeds confidence in your ability. You know it was a one off thing and you are better than that.

Do you think about/watch football in your spare time?

Yes, I like to watch the big games. That is the level that goalkeepers, or any professional footballer, strives to get to - otherwise you wouldn't be in the game.

I like to see the guys at the top of the game, at the top level and watch the keepers to see what they are about and what they are capable of. I try and work those sort of things into my game. So I think it is important to watch the big games at the top level.

Are there days you dislike football? Have you ever been close to quitting the game?

No, I have never been close to quitting. There are some days where you have had a bad training session and it gets to you sometimes. Obviously we do it every day of the week so it is a repetitive thing but I love the game and I would never think of quitting unless I had a serious injury or something else that was out of my control. That would be the only time I would think about quitting I would imagine.

What's the worst injury you've ever had?

Touch wood I have never had a bad injury. The worst thing I have done is pull a hamstring taking a goal kick in my first year in pro football. I was taking a goal kick in one of the games and my hamstring pulled up but I was only out for a week and missed one game. Touch wood I won't get any serious injuries in my career.

Is nutrition important to you?

I think nutrition is a big, big part of the game at the moment. Every club has their own nutritionist and it has had a massive impact on the game. I think a lot of athletes buy into it and try and fuel their bodies in the right way. I have bought into the idea. I think it is important to eat healthily and correctly. At the end of the day, it is what works for you really. If you eat stuff that makes you feel good then fine but I think you should give yourself the best opportunity you can, and fuel your body with the right things.

Do you do much in terms of strength training and plyometrics? How important is this to you?

I am quite a lean guy really so I'm quite skinny and tall, like 6ft 3, so it is a big part, to get stronger. I am not naturally a big, monstrous muscley guy but I like to make up for that with my agility and decision making and stuff like that. But it is a big part - we do like one or two sessions a week on weights and stuff and in my own time I go and do some sessions. It is important.

How often do you practice distribution? How important do you think distribution is in the modern game?

Yes it is a massive part of the game for goalkeepers nowadays. You only have to watch the Premiership with the likes of Pepe Reina and the side volley. I like to use the technique myself, it was something I picked up when I was 16. Growing up, at Reading as a scholar, I used to watch games and there was a goalie called Marcus Hahnemann who is playing at Wolves now. He used to use it, and it is a lethal tool to have because you can take a cross, get to the edge of the area and quickly hit a side volley to the channel for a winger and you are on the attack. So it is a massive tool for goalkeepers to have these days. It is an adaptable tool to have in your armoury.

Do you believe your talents were a product of genetics or through hard work? Or both?

I think a bit of both really. I believe you have to be naturally half decent at something to go and be successful at doing that, but obviously by the same token, you need to work hard at your game. Training takes you to the stage where you are ready to compete at professional football, that is what the training goes into, working on your technique in all aspects of goalkeeping, from communication all the way through to distribution.

Hard work is a big thing and that is what the coaches are there for. They teach you as long as you are willing to listen and work hard, then you should have a great chance of progression.

What is your biggest motivation?

For me it is to make my family proud. They gave me all the support I needed growing up. They drove me all around the country and watched me play wherever I was and I want to give something back to them really.

Appendix B

What's the biggest bit of advice you have for young keepers?

If you enjoy being a goalkeeper and it is something you want to pursue then you just need to really enjoy training whenever you can and listen to coaches. They have the experience and they are willing to help you. Just listen, enjoy yourself and try not to take it too seriously growing up. That is when problems start to happen, when you take it too seriously at a young age. You get to a certain level at 15, 16 and other things take part in your life where your friends are going out and stuff, and you want to be involved as well. Just try and enjoy it and when it gets to that level at 16 or so then you need to start taking it seriously then you get to a professional club.

Tom Heaton (Cardiff FC)

What age did you start playing in goal?

I first started playing in goal as an eight year old for a local club football team. The goalkeeper didn't want to play in goal anymore so I went from an outfield player, from centre midfield, to goalkeeper.

How did you get spotted?

At the time I was 10 or 11-years-old playing in as many teams as I could at the time – the school team, the local Sunday league team, the Chester Town team and I was also with the Wrexham School of Excellence (actually as an outfield player and a goalkeeper). There were no games at that time and it was just training so we ended up playing a game for Chester School Boys in Manchester where a Man United scout spotted me. I came for a trial a couple of months later and signed then.

What is the reason you wanted to be a goalkeeper?

Honestly, at the time I was playing in a very poor local club team, and the outfield wasn't really doing a lot for me so I decided to go in goal for a bit of action. I had previously quite enjoyed doing it and it went from there really.

I found out I was fairly decent in goal and enjoyed it, so I went from there really and tried to get a bit better at it, and I did.

My trial for Man United came as a goalkeeper so that made my decision for me. When I signed - that was me going to be a goalkeeper.

Appendix B

Who was your idol and why?

I signed at Man United as an 11-year-old, at the time it was definitely Peter Schmeichel. The way he played and the way he kept the ball out of the net was incredible to me at the time and still is to be fair. So, it was definitely Peter Schmeichel. I used to try and model the things he did.

Was there anyone in your life who was particularly influential?

Yes I have a fantastic support network around me with my girlfriend and my family. My dad has always been there so it would be fair to say my dad. Since I first started playing he took me to training three or four times a week. I cannot remember the last football game he missed whether it is abroad or at different places around the country. He has been instrumental for me.

How did you do in school? Do you have any advice on education for young keepers?

I always fairly enjoyed school and I quite liked trying to be good academically as well. Obviously football was always a massive part, especially growing up and as I got older I went down to a four-day week at school. If you can offer a young boy in Year 10 a four-day week, and one day playing football (as well as the weekends playing football) then they would snap your hand off, and I obviously did.

I think it is always best to work as hard as you can and be the best you can be at everything you do. I tried to apply that to my school work and everything around that, and I used to enjoy it.

What has been your greatest football-related experience?

Three spring to mind really. I was fortunate to be in the 24-man squad that went to Moscow in 2008 in the Champions League final which obviously Man United won. I didn't make the bench that day but I was third choice goalie for the day which is obviously a fantastic experience being in and around the dressing room with the lads.

Starting for the Under-21s over in Spain also sticks out. We played Columbia at Malaga Stadium which is obviously a big achievement for me starting for the Under-21s.

On top of that I came on in a European XI game where Man United played a European XI at Old Trafford for the second half in front of 75,000 which was great for me. I think it would be those three that stick out.

What's your best ever save and why?

Good question. I would probably say, I played for Cardiff at the Emirates Stadium against Arsenal and we got beat 4-0 but I actually had quite a decent game and there was a save where the ball has come in and Vela has brought it down and hit a shot and I blocked it on the line and the ball fell to Bendtner. He hit it against the post, the ball came back to him and I dived and I managed to keep his second attempt out. It was one of those that wasn't a textbook save, or what you would expect a keeper to do, but it was so unorthodox and it didn't look like I was going to be able to save it. So it was up there with one of the best I have done.

What is your mind-set prior to games? Do you get nervous? How do you deal with it?

I used to be quite an intense character before games. I quickly realised that wasn't really working for me in a sense. If you want to perform at your best at any sport, or anything you do, then I think you have to have a concentration and a focus on what you want to achieve. But I think you need to be in a state where you can perform at your best, and that intensity wasn't working for me. So I changed it. I am now a lot more relaxed prior to games and around the dressing room no matter what the occasion.

Obviously I am still focused on the job, and ready to go if you like, but still being fairly relaxed and taking on the mind-set of enjoy the challenge of what you want to do.

At the end of the day you are playing a football match, you are where you want to be, everyone who has played football wants to be there, they have wanted it and they have earned it and enjoying the challenge of beating your opponent. So I try and take that into the games these days and have that more relaxed approach.

Do you analyse your performance after the game?

Yes, I used to do it more so than I do now but I used to be a little bit intense where I perhaps did too much of that. Obviously I still do it to an extent because there are certainly things you can learn from. Well, lots you can learn from, by looking back at games at what you did and what you need to improve on. What you are good at but still need to work at.

I am definitely in favour of analysing your game and seeing what you can improve on and I am definitely one that does that.

How do you deal with mistakes? Does it ruin your weekend?

It used to, it certainly doesn't any more. I think what you have to accept, particularly as a goalkeeper is that mistakes will happen, it is part of the position. You want to try and minimise them but there has to be an acceptance that it will happen at some stage.

People are only human, you are not going to make the right decisions all the time and not going to do the right thing all the time. Obviously strive to do it all the time but for me once it happens these days, you put it down to a learning experience, you move on. If you have the mind-set that you are trying to do the right thing all the time, and you make a mistake while you are trying to do the right thing, then I think you will minimise the mistakes and do more good than bad. I think *that* is the mindset I try and take forward.

Obviously it is not nice when you make mistakes but you need broad shoulders and you need to take it on the chin and show your character and come out fighting.

Do you think about/watch football in your spare time?

Very much so. I love football, it is something that I have always loved and always wanted to be involved in. I very much eat, sleep and breathe it to be fair. A lot of people are different but that is the way I have always done it and I quite enjoy doing it that way.

There is obviously a time to put the ball away, if you like, and do something else whether it be golf or days out doing something different. There is certainly a time to do that but if I am in the house and there is a game on then I know what I will be watching.

Are there days you dislike football? Have you ever been close to quitting the game?

No, not personally, I have to be honest. It has never crossed my mind at all. I have always enjoyed the challenge if there is a hurdle in the way or pressure on your shoulders or you feel a bit stressed. I have always enjoyed the challenge of shaking it off and looking to the light at the end of the tunnel so I have never had feelings like that, and I hope I never do.

Appendix B

What's the worst injury you've ever had? Was it hard to come back?

Yes, it was actually. I played an England Under-16 game at Leicester's stadium in 2001 against Germany Under-16s and I had a triple fracture mandible, which is a broken jaw in three places. A guy kneed me in the face and I was out for a long time with that – two operations and metal plates in the side of my jaw - at an age when I had just gone full time with Man United. I was improving every day and it set me back a little. It was four or five months and then I dislocated a finger which set me back another month or so and all in all, before I got back to where I wanted to be, it was almost a year. It almost took 12 months out of my development.

But looking back, those are the times you learn and realise that you have to work for what you want, you don't just fall into success. You have to pull your finger out if you like and strive towards your goal every day. So that was what I did and it helped me realise that.

Is nutrition important to you?

Yes very much so. I have always wanted to eat the right things and never been a big drinker at all. Nowadays I am trying to get even better again. Obviously it is so important, what you eat is what you are - they say. It is vitally important. If you fuel your body with the wrong stuff then you will never get the best out of yourself and I have always been an advocate of making every percent count. Nutrition is a big chunk of that percentage. I think it is fair to say that it is something that every professional footballer should be required to look at and be required to do.

Do you do much in terms of strength training/plyometrics?

Yes, I have done an awful lot of that. Just this summer actually I have spent a lot of time with some excellent coaches up in the north, at a place called the Underground Train Station, which is a new gym just emerging. It is like a warehouse gym in Hoylake on the Wirral, which isn't too far from my mum and dad's house. It has been excellent really. It has a lot of Olympic lifting as well as plyometics and sprinting, and it just helps you get prepared.

Goalkeeping is an explosive position, it is not about half an hour runs, or 20 minute runs, it is about explosive movements at the right time and short sprints and quick movements. It is important to train for that to improve it. I have done a lot of work on that over the years and I am still doing so.

How often do you practice distribution?

Every day. These days it is one of those big things that is becoming more and more important. If you can distribute the ball well, or better than most, then managers are going to look at that and want you in the team. I think there are some fantastic distributors of the ball in the game at the minute and it is important to do it; left foot, right foot, volley, half volley, goal kicks, it is so important to get all those things right and it requires practice. No one steps up to the ball and can hit an accurate diagonal just by chance. It is one of those things that takes a lot of practice and a lot of work and requires 10, 15, 20 minutes every day, minimum, to be honest.

Do you think it's essential to be tall to be a keeper in the modern game? What advice do you have for keepers who have experienced height related setbacks?

I think it helps but I have never been a fan of putting height down as a stumbling block. The fact is if you are good enough then you are big enough. I think you have to find other ways to battle on - you need good spring if you are not the biggest, you will need to be strong, and your decisions will need to be better than a lad who is bigger. Although height is something which is perhaps helpful, it is by no means a necessity in my opinion.

Do you believe your talents were a product of genetics or through hard work?

I think it is through hard work. I think everyone is genetically different, some people get more than others but I think it is fair to say that hard work is something I have certainly put in through the years - and will hopefully carry on doing that. I think it is important to do it as early as you can, as much as you can, and if you think outside the box a little bit then the rewards pay off in the end.

What is your biggest motivation?

Good question. My biggest motivation is my career goal. My career goal is to play for England and be England's number one. With that in the back of my mind, obviously you break that down and to be England's number one, you have to play in the Premiership. So I start breaking down like that really. I think that, at the end of the day, drives me on and that is where I want to get to. That is what I am striving for and that is what I am working for every day.

So when it is raining and muddy outside, although I actually like those days, use it as an analogy for now, they are the days I have in the back of my mind and that is what drives me on and gives me the determination to keep working towards it.

What's the biggest bit of advice you have for young keepers?

My biggest bit of advice is to work hard. The more time you give to it, the more you get out of it. It may seem like a very simple concept but it often gets misplaced and misguided and missed, if you like. I think the fact is, if you do more than everyone else then you give yourself a much better chance than everyone else.

That is certainly the philosophy I try to work by. The more time you put in, the more you give yourself a good chance to get to where you want to go.

Appendix C
Web Links

To see video highlights of this memorable season please visit
www.socceredits.com

My personal websites

www.RichardLeeGK.com

This website includes stats, video footage and pictures of my
football career to date.

www.RichardLeeNLP.com

Interested in hiring me for coaching or for a speaking
arrangement? If so find details here on what I can offer.

Appendix C

www.RichardLeeMV.com

I supply the health drink MonaVie, a drink that I now take religiously and one that has had a huge impact on my energy levels and in turn performance, therefore I became a distributor! If you're interested in buying MonaVie or becoming a distributor then visit this site and get in touch.

www.gkicon.com

My goalkeeping business, we have goalkeeping schools all over the UK so if you are a goalkeeper looking for coaching then please do check the website for a venue near you. If you are a goalkeeper coach looking to start up your own goalkeeping business then we have a fantastic franchise package which can help you do just that.

www.drcap.co.uk

On the back of our infamous appearance on Dragons' Den I'm pleased to say that Dr Cap continues to go from strength to strength. Satisfy all your headwear needs here!

www.everyoneneedsamentor.com

My latest project and one that I'm quite passionate about. I know that my mentors have had an incredible effect on my life and with this website we look to match up those who want to improve in their chosen field with a suitable mentor who has already succeeded in that very field. Come and find that someone who can help unlock your potential.

www.RichardLeePC.com

I plan to take on a few footballers who I can help coach personally, if you are a professional footballer and are interested in hiring me as your 'performance coach' then please visit my website and I'd be happy to speak to you about how I intend to operate and how I could help you reach new levels of excellence.

www.sportingconnect.com

A new business with the intention of helping players find quality coaches in their area.

www.refuelstore.com

My dad's business - including world famous brands such as Mitchell & Ness, and Starter.

Social Networks

Facebook: www.Facebook.com/RichardLeeGK

Twitter: @rleegk

Lightning Source UK Ltd.
Milton Keynes UK
UKHW010943160419
341105UK00010BA/770/P